First published 2010 by Boxtree
an imprint of Pan Macmillan Ltd
Pan Macmillan, 20 New Wharf Road, London N1 9RR
Basingstoke and Oxford
Associated companies throughout the world
www.panmacmillan.com

ISBN 978-0-7522-2736-8

A CIP catalogue record for this book is available from the British Library.

Design by Estuary English
Printed and bound by L.E.G.O. SpA, Italy

# NEXT YEAR'S BOOK

## ALL-NEW
# SCENES WE'D
# LIKE TO SEE

**EWAN PHILLIPS, DAN PATTERSON, SIMON BULLIVANT,
ROB COLLEY, DAN GASTER, GED PARSONS, GILES
PILBROW, STEVE PUNT AND COLIN SWASH**

BOXTREE

# CONTENTS

# 1. UNLIKELY DICTIONARY DEFINITIONS (Part 1)

**abstract** (*adj.*): hard to explain really, so why not just look it up? Oh.

**arsehopper** (*n.*): small green insect that lives up your arse. I may have misheard this.

**badger** *(n.)*: massive fire-breathing predator with huge teeth, extremely dangerous, must be stopped. Do you hear me? We're not safe! Why does no one listen?

**balls** (*n., pl.*): what does it mean if they start to go flakey and red? I'm getting worried. Any doctors reading this?

**cheese** (*n.*) 1. a small dangerous flying insect, as in 'I have just been stung by a cheese.' 2. character in Shakespeare's Henry V: 'My noble Lord Cheese, at the double to Gloucester.' 3. what my wife complains my feet smell of, like hers smell of roses or something. 4. type of martial art.

**Claire Wilson** (*pr.*): girl who I really fancied at school, I always told her I'd be famous one day. See? Look Claire, I'm writing the dictionary. I suppose you married that bloke who played for the football team? If not email me at oed.com and send pics …

**close** (*adj.*): near, adjacent, as in 'You're sitting too close too me. Look, I'm trying to write the dictionary, could you give me some space?'

**coconut** (*n.*): hard-shelled fruit of palm trees. Looks like a big testicle. 1. 'Doctor, doctor, I've got a coconut up my arse.' 2. 'Ow! That fucking coconut you threw at me really hurt, you stupid childish c**t. Fuck off, Steven.' 3. err … 'I've got a lovely bunch of coconuts.' 4. um … 'Is that a coconut or a car I can see over there?' 'What? It's a car.' 5. 'Hello, is that Colin the Coconut?' 'It is, yeah.' 'OK … right.' 6. Energy = mass times coconut squared or something.

**date** (*n.*): romantic assignation such as dinner or the theatre that usually ends with an awkward departure at the Tube, or a pathetic, groping attempt to force yourself on her before strangling the life out of her to make yourself feel clean again.

**disinterested** (*adj.*): to have no interest in, neutral, as in not biased or having an interest. Not to be confused with uninterested as it generally is by most of you ignorant fuckers out there.

**earth** (*n.*): the planet we live on. Come on, do you really need to look this up?

**ejaculate** (*v.*): to exclaim or say out loud with a mouthful of semen, e.g. 'Oh, that was good!' Peter ejaculated.

**embezzlement** (*n.*): look, I was found not guilty, can you stop bringing this up and we can just move on.

**feelings** (*n.*): you know when you like feel stuff and that you know.

**fluppertupperflumarummadum** (*n.*): the noise that a fart I did on a leather chair in the office this morning made. I've never made a sound like that before, do you think I have something wrong with me?

**gay** (*adj.*): I'm not. Why? That was just an isolated incident at university. I was confused.

**gullible** (*adj.*): if you look this up in the dictionary, there's a picture of you. Ha ha! Look! Oh …

# 2. LINES YOU WON'T FIND IN AN ENID BLYTON BOOK

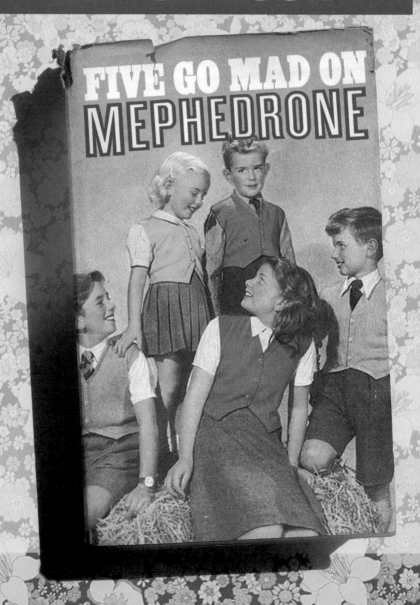

FIVE GO MAD ON MEPHEDRONE

Anne found Dick's limp, headless body chained to a lamppost with the message: 'Stay off our patch. The Secret Seven'.

'I don't think I'm going to be in this story when the book is reprinted in the 1970s,' said Mr Golliwog the train driver.

'Remember, Noddy,' warned PC Plod, 'if anyone asks, you fell down the stairs.'

'Now I'm hoping you seven live up to your name. Mum's the word,' said Uncle Basil, zipping up his flies, winking and putting his finger to his lips.

George, Anne, Julian and Dick looked on in surprise as the drugs baron whipped out an Uzi and blew them all away.

'Right!' said George. 'This summer's Mystery is to find out who got Anne pregnant!'

'Bring Timmy,' said Julian, 'I'm sure he'll love whatever this "dogging" is they do up at the old farm building.'

'Come on. Our work is done,' said Anne. 'Let's get home and celebrate with twenty Lambert & Butler, a tube of Pringles and lashings of cheap, super-strength cider.'

Aunt Fanny was clearly tiring of the Five's childish laughter every time her name was mentioned and had taken to slyly torturing Timmy.

'I'm afraid you can't call gypsy Jo a pikey any more, Dick,' said Anne primly.

'Anne and I are feeling very gay today Julian … and we'd like you to donate your sperm for our child, please,' said George butchly.

'This holiday,' said Julian, 'the Famous Five will find out what lies behind the current spate of teenage stabbings.'

And kindly old PC Barratt cycled away gaily, saying, 'Those silly children, there's nothing remotely suspicious going on at the old bin Laden farm.'

And so they put Timmy in a sack, threw him in the canal and said, 'Right, we're the Famous Four now.'

# 3. UNLIKELY THINGS TO READ ON THE BACK OF A BOOK (Part 1)

'I literally shat myself' – *New York Times*

'I wouldn't buy this book even if it offered me a blow-job every hour on the hour for life'

'I have a copy of *War and Peace* permanently by the side of my bed. How else would I get in?' – Ronnie Corbett

*Harry Potter and the Abused Vampire Girl With a Dragon Tattoo* is a desperate attempt by J. K. Rowling to put all the elements of a bestselling book into one publication. She also throws in a couple of recipes and a diet.

If comedy is the new rock 'n' roll, then Syd Little is surely Buddy Holly (and not just because he wears glasses!). Read his fascinating life story as Syd tickles your funny bone and opens up your tear ducts in *Little by Little* with a foreword by Roger de Courcey and Nookie Bear … Shit! We advanced him £500,000 for this, I thought we'd got Michael McIntyre, I'm finished …

'I got through Dan Brown's book in one sitting, admittedly this was sitting on the toilet after a particularly runny shit without any toilet paper'

'I didn't have time to read it'

'Unusually good-quality paper'

ISBN 978-1-84854-103-0

£7.99

'I hate my life'

'More drama and thrills than driving a Toyota'

'Complete and utter bollocks' – *Guardian*

'*Fiscal Accountancy Part Four* is a rollocking good read' – Gordon Brown

'Kept me guessing right till the end when I found out the policeman did it'

'If I had to recommend one Kerry Katona novel it would be this one'

'If you only read one book this year – you're thick'

'This book kept me sane' – Amy Winehouse

*The Very Horny Chihuahua* is a very different sort of book from the author of *The Very Hungry Caterpillar*

'As good as anything written by Brown, King or Forsyth, though I am of course referring to Gordon Brown, Ledley King and Bruce Forsyth'

'Proust's *À la Recherche du Temps Perdu* is a breathtaking tour de force, and rightfully occupies its iconic place as the key roman-fleuve in the Western literary tradition' – Jedward

'If you can read this, you're too close'

'Sith' – *Dyslexic Weekly*

ISBN 978-1-84854-103-0

£7.99

# 4. UNLIKELY BOARD-GAME INSTRUCTIONS (Part 1)

Having taken the cards out of your rectum, shuffle them and give everyone the maximum they will accept.

Give each player a red or green counter at the start.
DO NOT open the vial of smallpox yet.

To begin, insert phallus into the opponent of your choice.

Oh, I don't know. I didn't think this through properly.

You have lost. Alter your will in favour of Waddingtons.

Sit on the shoulders of the person to your left. You are now
ready to begin.

New Kerwank! Each player takes it in turn to place more and
more fingers around the shaft. Whoever is holding it when it
goes off loses.

Three players sit around the board, the fourth is dangled out of
the window.

Spin the chamber, put gun to temple, pull trigger. If you are still
alive, pass the gun to the next player on your left.

Set the timer to three minutes or three years. These are the only
units of time allowed.

Choose an opponent and out them as a homosexual.

If you land on a ladder you go up. If you land on a snake you go
down, if you know what I mean, luv.

The cocaine should be divided into six lines of equal length using
the mirror and credit card provided. The Bank then awards each
player a rolled up note and the game can begin!

# 5. UNLIKELY TV LISTINGS

**1.00 p.m. FILM: Another Day Gone**
Classic black-and-white British film no one remembers starring John Mills as a teacher in a Devon village during the war. Not very good and you'll hate yourself for sitting through it all and wasting another day of your pointless, miserable, fast disappearing existence.

**2.30 p.m. FILM: Charlie's Anals**
In a disastrous mix-up by their rights buyers, ITV accidentally screen the porn version of *Charlie's Angels* as their big Easter blockbuster. Coincidentally also starring Drew Barrymore though.

**4.00 p.m. Come Fight With Me**
Mouthy cockney barrow-boy Johnno hosts a tear-up between a Geordie former squaddie, a Scouse drug dealer and a touchy traffic warden.

**4.30 p.m. The Divine Mr Cameron**
The baby-faced Tory talks us through his education policy with the help of a spicy Thai soup, explains his tax cuts through the medium of crab cakes with chilli jam and crème fraiche, and rounds off by showing how to curb immigration using ice cream, chocolate sauce and spiced plums.

**5.00 p.m. Search for the Ripper**
Graham Norton and Andrew Lloyd Webber audition hopefuls for the role of Jack the Ripper in the new west End musical *Naughty Jack*. Judges, as ever, are Jamelia, Michael Crawford, Chief Superintendent David Hatcher and Rose West.

**5.30 p.m. Total Wipeout**
After getting hit on the head by a tennis ball, Richard Hammond relapses and forgets everything apart from the word 'chaffinch' and the smell of WD-40.

**6.00 p.m. FILM: Meet One's Parents**
(1955, b/w, comedy)
The long-forgotten Ealing Studios original of the Ben Stiller movie, starring Ian Carmichael as Rumpy Pillock, the prospective son-in-law anxious to make an impression at the home of girlfriend Sylvia Syms' parents, played by James Robertson Justice and Hattie Jacques. Leslie Phillips plays the ex-boyfriend and Alfie Bass blacks up as the gamekeeper 'Darkie'.

**7.30 p.m. Embarrassing Bodies: John Prescott Special**
Episode 1 of 125.

**8.00 p.m. FILM: The Same Old Kooky Bollocks**
'Comedy' where Jennifer Aniston and Jason Bateman star as exes stranded on a sleeper train in Kansas as they try to get home to their individual engagement parties, or some shit like that, don't ask me, I've only seen this because I was on

a date with that bird with the massive baps who works in Subway in Watford and heard she'd probably put out on the first night. Actually that may even have been another Aniston film, they're all the fucking same.

### 9.30 p.m. Pile of Shite
New series of the sitcom everyone assumed would be quietly cancelled after series one. Tonight Susan Shite decides living upstairs from her mother-in-law and underneath her ex-husband is putting a strain on the relationship with her new husband or something rubbish.

*Susan Shite* Caroline Quentin
*Agatha Shite* Celia Imrie
*Alan* That bloke off the advert for the thing
*Himself* R Kelly
*Bill Shite* Sir Ben Kingsley

### 10.00 p.m. Yentob: Live and Unstoppable
BBC2 presents an evening of near-the-knuckle stand-up, ribald song and dance routines and thoughtful lectures on modern art from the stubbly exec at a vast, echoingly empty Royal Albert Hall.

### 10.30 p.m. Grey's Anatomy
Live from New York's Roosevelt Hospital, a gynaecological examination of former *Dirty Dancing* actress Jennifer Grey.

### 11.00 p.m. Panorama
Tonight, are current affairs programmes dumbing down? A thought-provoking examination from Bobby Davro and the girl who plays Rosie Webster in *Coronation Street*, with music from The Saturdays.

### 11.30 p.m. Leon's Bidet
Baffling seven-hour drama from Steven Poliakoff starring Michael Gambon, Saskia Reeves and former Coventry City defender Brian Kilcline as people sitting about in big houses looking sad and occasionally crying.

### 12.00 a.m. Question Time
David Dimbleby presents a *Question Time C\*\*ts' Special* live from Hemel Hempstead, with guests Richard Littlejohn, Diane Abbott, George Galloway, Nigel Farage and Piers Morgan.

### 12.30 a.m. Cooking With Twats: The Bloody Lovely Mr Brown
Comedian Roy Chubby Brown cooks black pudding, tripe and gravy in soft-focus lighting, pausing every now and again to tell a questionable joke about a Pakistani and a nun.

### 1.00 a.m. Later ... with Jools Holland
In an extended edition of Tuesday's show, Jools is joined in the plunge pool by John Leslie, Vernon Kay, Hardeep Singh Kohli and a group of teenage cheerleaders from Holland.

### 1.30 a.m. Justin Lee Collins: Good Times
Well, at least he's enjoying himself.

### 2.00 a.m. Peter Kay Year
The beginning of 365 days of whatever the self-effacing, roly-poly Boltonian feels like putting on Channel 4.

### 3.00 a.m. DIY LOL
Nick Knowles and the team visit the houses of people who have recently done Do It Yourself and mercilessly take the piss out of their terrible efforts.

# 6. UNLIKELY THINGS TO READ IN A ROMANCE NOVEL

It was love at first sight – she a beautiful heiress, he a donkey with a hat.

He pulled down his trousers to reveal his throbbing manhood. 'It's been throbbing like that since I shagged the chambermaid,' he said.

He took her in his arms, his roving hands tracing her delicate curves till at last they closed upon her throbbing – phallus? Oh my God, it's a man …

As the night drew in, she kissed his lips and they parted. She climbed inside her luxurious four-poster bed and he trudged back to his kennel.

He unbuttoned his tunic and trousers and found himself donning a condom before thrusting himself into her where it was all over in literally seconds.

They met as if it were ordained in the stars, as if the very gods themselves had bade it happen; it was at a sales conference at a hotel in Solihull.

Slowly, methodically, he began to lick the glistening honey from her quivering body. Suddenly, he stopped and, lifting his head, he roared, 'Urrgghh! I've got a pube in my throat. Yuk!'

'Don't put it up there, luv, I had a curry last night.'

'But my lord, how will I know if I give my maidenhead to thee now, if you take my innocence in a burst of passion, that you will not forget my sacrifice when you return from the wars in France?'
 'Alright then, you could just wank us off?' he said.

Sonya fell into his arms and he let rip: 'Oops, followed through there, I'm afraid.'

She felt the blood pumping through her heart – and his cock.

As he pulled her towards him she could feel his heart beat next to hers. That's strange, she thought, his heart's on the wrong side of his body.

There was something about him that told her instantly that he was Mr Right. It was his name badge. He was called 'Frank Right'.

She swooned in his arms. 'Let me feel the throbbing urgency of your desire.'
   'Do you mean cock, love? Well why didn't you just say?'

Her heart raced as he went down on one knee in front of her. Juan Knee was the first half-Spanish half-Thai ladyboy she'd ever seen.

As they lay back, all passion spent, she heard those three little words in her ear: 'Tea please, luv.'

She stepped out of the bathroom in just her nightie, stood in the moonlight and whispered tenderly, 'I'd give that ten minutes if I were you.'

As he held her passionately in his arms, she whispered into his ear: 'It's an extra tenner for anal.'

Lady Rothermere swooned as she told him: 'I'll have to suck you off, I've got the painters in.'

Charles tenderly held her in his arms as Annabel chucked up her seven Bacardi breezers.

Lord Huffington and Lord Darcy had first met at the spit roast of Lady Westlake.

# 7. UNLIKELY THINGS TO READ IN A SCHOOL TEXTBOOK

Insert the straw into the frog's anus and blow.

Sir Isaac Newton discovered the laws of repulsion by marrying the ugliest bird in the village.

Insert penis A into vagina B and geography teacher C gets fired.

Take the distilled solution of methyl alcohol – add ice, lemon and drink.

If Emile Heskey kicks the ball at the goal from a distance of five yards, how far back in Row Z will it land?

Question: What is O2 the symbol for?
Answer: A phone that doesn't work.

Exercise One:
Please write 'Sir is a bender' on every page of this book.

Chemistry – What's that smell?

The female body is significantly different to a male's as it was made out of a rib.

There are well over one hundred elements, but only three of them are any good.

The periodic table goes as follows: hydrogen, helium, lithium, unobtanium.

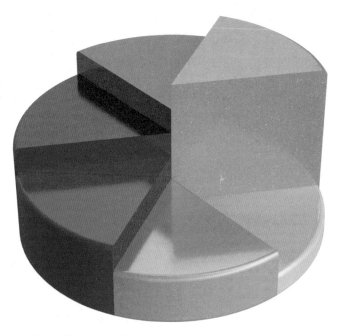

Foreword by Timmy Mallett.

It's hot in here, said the young blonde science mistress as she slowly unbuttoned her starched white lab coat …

The formation of an oxbow lake is a piece of knowledge which will prove invaluable to you for the rest of your life.

The atomic symbol for lead is … oh, it doesn't matter, you're all going to get an A* anyway.

The French for 'Where is the supermarket?' is 'WHERE … IS … SUPERMARKET?'

Henry VIII was a fat bastard with syphilis. Discuss.

# 8. UNLIKELY HEALTH AND SAFETY ADVICE (Part 1)

WARNING: IN THE EVENT OF FIRE, RUN LIKE FUCK

IF A WORKMATE HAS FAINTED, ON NO ACCOUNT POUR SULPHURIC ACID ON THE BODY

IN THE EVENT OF FIRE, TAKE TIME TO BE AWARE OF COLLEAGUES WHO MAY REQUIRE ASSISTANCE AND GET OUT BEFORE THEY DO. LET THE WEAK GO TO THE WALL!

IF A WORK COLLEAGUE IS INJURED, LOOSEN CLOTHING AND THEN GO AND LOOSEN THEIRS, YOU'LL NEVER GET A BETTER OPPORTUNITY

SEMTEX: DO NOT PLACE UP ARSE

PLACE ENCLOSED CAPSULE UNDER YOUR TEETH. ONLY SWALLOW IF CAPTURED BY ALLIED FORCES

CHAIRS CAN BE LETHAL

IN THE EVENT OF A COLLEAGUE SUSTAINING SERIOUS INJURY, KEEP PUNCHING UNTIL THE C*NT LEARNS HIS LESSON

ON NO ACCOUNT TAKE TWO BOTTLES INTO THE SHOWER. PLEASE REMEMBER, JUST WASH AND GO

THE BRINGING OF CHEESE ONTO THESE PREMISES IS EXPRESSLY VERBOTEN

STRICTLY NO COME DANCING

FUCK FUCK FUCK FUUUUUUCCCCKKKK!

IN THE EVENT OF JEWISH OR GREEK WEDDINGS, BREAK GLASS

NUCLEAR MISSILES. DANGER: DO NOT STORE NEXT TO OPEN FLAME

# 9. UNLIKELY THINGS TO READ IN A PARISH MAGAZINE (Part 1)

Parish Notices

'Revved Up': This week the vicar uses his hard-hitting column to explain why he thinks Sharia law would work in Chipping-under-Widdlewood.

Helga, 24 yrs, Swedish, new in town 36-24-26.

Father Brian's racing tip: Suffolk Boy 3.45 at Southwell, Tuesday 24th. 'Fourteen to one, get on it.'

Speakers at St Botulph's Hall this month: Richard Dawkins, Marilyn Manson and Ian Huntley.

Sinner of the Month: Mrs Jones from 44 The Grove has been self-pleasuring whilst her husband is away in France. She asked for some swearing, selfishness and a handful of mildly racist thoughts when driving to be dealt with too. Vote Now for a) Three Our Fathers, Two Hail Marys and a Glory Be, b) Two Our Fathers, Two Hail Marys and an act of charity, or c) Excommunication from the Parish.

Breaking News … There is no God.

'I'M GAY' SAYS VICAR, MORE INSIDE PAGES 2–7.

Join us on Sunday at 2 p.m. at the Village Hall for tea, cake and a welcome party for the gypsies currently residing outside.

A message from Ian, the master of 1st Tiddleswood Cubs and Scouts: 'Thanks to everyone for their support during my recent trial. Six boys will be rewarded with their Fabricating DNA Evidence badges at the Scout Hut on Thursday evening at 7.30 p.m.'

**FOR SALE:** Religious artefacts, miracle cures, forgiveness for sins, entrance to the Kingdom of Heaven.

Christmas Fancy Dress Party: 'Tarts and Vicars' theme.

Church Hall Happy Hour: Alcopops £1, free shorts with any guest beer between 7 and 8 p.m. Friday night.

Wicked Whisper: Which tall, dark parishioner told me in confession he's been having an affair with the neighbour two doors down? His wife might just 'butcher' him when she finds out.

Cats Protection: Give us £25 or Tiddles loses a fucking paw. Call usual number.

This week's recycle dates: Friday 2nd: paper, bottles, cardboard. Saturday 3rd: syringes, condoms and tampons.

Anyone for Tango? 'Tango' comes to town at the Bob Norman Centre from April 18th every Wednesday at 7.30 p.m. No dance experience necessary. Singles or couples welcome. For more information or to reserve your place ring 01909 12312346 or email dogging@fuckinginpublic.com, website: www.pretendthisistango.co.uk.

Midsomer Parish Magazine: A list of this week's murder victims to pray for.

A special thanks to both of you who took part in the 24 Hour 'Earth' Event to raise green awareness last Friday. Cheers Bill and Sandra, much appreciated.

Ibbledon Choral Society present 'Fuck You, I Won't Do What You Tell Me', an evening of tribute to Rage Against the Machine and Slayer at 8 p.m. on Wednesday. Tea and fucking scones provided.

February weather statistics: the total rainfall for the month was 86.5 mm (3.4 in.), having rained on 19 days. This was significantly more than the rainfall in the same month last year: 57 mm (2.24 in.) and not a patch on me and my partner José, as I got the full 241 mm (9.5 in.) on all 28 days thank you very much. Olé!

# 10. UNPLEASANT CRISP FLAVOURS
## (Part 1)

**Really**
**OVERPOWERINGLY**
**FISHY**
CRISPS
*No artificial flavours, colours or MSG*

NATURALLY LOW IN

Each bag contains

| Saturates | Salt |
| 0.8g | 0.3g |
| | 5% |

SALT AND SEAMAN

CHEESE AND BUNION

HALE AND PACE

BURNT RUBBER

PETROL

BREAST MILK AND CHIVES

PISS AND CHIPS

GROUND GLASS AND BLOOD

BURP AND VOMIT

BATSHIT, CATSHIT AND RATSHIT

TARTS AND VICARS

BEEF CURTAINS

GRAPES AND WRATH

RED HOT CHILI PEPPERS

COW DUNG

# 11. UNLIKELY THINGS TO HEAR DURING A SCHOOL ASSEMBLY

'And the prize for Most Fondled Bottom goes to Tompkins.'

'This year's Speech Day has of course been ruined by those silly boys who assassinated Mr Bartram.'

'Good morning, collected scum and fuckwits ...'

'For being caught with cocaine, Simkins of 4B will be given 100 lines.'

'Now Johnson is going to make an appeal for your money, whilst Hargreaves threatens you with a knife and Parsons films it on his mobile phone.'

'As I look out on a sea of brilliant young faces, I can't help picturing myself skinny dipping in it, gulping down lungfuls of adolescent pheremones.'

'Now if I could ask Fortescue Minor and his hoes to come up to the dais and tell us about the shit going down with his homies ...'

'And that was the story of "My First Wet Dream".'

'I have taught here now for forty years and I have to say: this year, you boys have made me realise how I have completely and utterly wasted my fucking life.'

'Other notable achievements this term: Anderson has had his first smoke and Johnson has lost his virginity.'

'And so to sum up, statistically most of you have no hope, so I suggest you just go outside and kill yourselves.'

'And to tell you about his lifelong struggle with illegal substances, Mr Porter the chemistry teacher.'

'James. Thurston. Jones. Harris. Harcourt. Wilson ... are the boys who are still missing, presumed dead.'

'Also on this term's bulletin board, Smithson won the Nobel Prize for Literature and Hughes was beheaded by al Qaeda.'

'And could I say before we begin that the good news is that Mr Beecham is back with his wife. The bad news therefore is that I am sleeping alone again.'

'Due to budgetary restraints, this term's Geography field-trip will be a trip to a field.'

'And because of the government's deliberate downgrading of our educational system, everyone got A stars, thus rendering them meaningless.'

'I remember when I was your age I used to have to walk three miles home before masturbating all afternoon.'

'Of course in my day, things were different. We had discipline, lots of it, administered by matron with her milk-white silken thighs, her cheap French perfume and her enormous ... excuse me, sorry, I need to lie down ...'

'And the Fourth Form science prize goes to Hamza for this booby trapped rucksack.'

'In line with our new policy of zero tolerance, for forgetting his gym kit Jenkins of 4C will be hanged in the playground during morning break.'

'Our guest speaker is someone I think will inspire you, probably our most famous old girl ... here she is ... Rosemary West.'

'Sixth Form students should note that leaving Miss Ferguson floating in a tank of formaldehyde was not only criminal, but was also marked down for being highly derivative.'

# 12. THINGS YOU WON'T HEAR FROM A FORMULA 1 COMMENTATOR

*'And he's pulling in for a piss!'*

*'All the drivers have their rituals. One of them's brought along a tiny good luck troll. Oh, my mistake – it's Bernie Ecclestone.'*

*'He's pulled in for new tyres and his pit crew have said it'll be Tuesday.'*

*'Extraordinary! He's asking for directions.'*

*'Nyow nyow, the race hasn't started yet, I'm just not very well.'*

*'Oh dear, he's got stuck behind an elderly couple out for a run.'*

*'Well, the British Grand Prix has been ruined by the government's installation of speed cameras on Hangar Straight.'*

'Hey! – That car just overtook another car.'

'Welcome back after that break – and while you were gone, nothing at all of any interest happened.'

'And they're off! – yes, Max Mosely's pants are off!'

'I don't know who's winning – they keep going too fast for me to see.'

'Bernie Ecclestone there with his very tall wife, and you can't help but wonder about the impracticalities of their sex life.'

'He's stopped at the zebra crossing and now a tractor has pulled out in front.'

'He's gone into the pits for a Ginsters pasty and a Lucozade.'

'Enjoy this race because after it there will be no more petrol left in the world.'

'I don't know who's going to win but I can tell you a Japanese guy in a shit car will come last.'

'Lewis Hamilton is first, followed by Frankie Dettori on Arab Boy.'

# 13. LINES YOU WON'T HEAR IN *STAR TREK*
## (Part 1)

'CAPTAIN, I DON'T LIKE BEING CALLED SPOCKFACE.'

'WHEN YOU BEAMED ME UP, I THINK I LOST MY COCK.'

'FULL SPEED AHEAD, MR TOLSTOY.'

'CAPTAIN'S CHOCOLATE LOG, USE BY DATE: CHRISTMAS 2052.'

'CLEAN ME UP, SCOTTY.'

'WE'VE REACHED THE MOON, CAPTAIN, I DON'T THINK WE SHOULD GO FURTHER.'

'BAD NEWS, CAPTAIN – DILITHIUM CRYSTALS DON'T EXIST.'

'OUR FAN BASE ARE ALL MIDDLE AGED WITH DISPOSABLE INCOMES – TO MAKE ANOTHER MOVIE WOULD BE LOGICAL, CAPTAIN.'

'SENSOR READINGS INDICATE ANOTHER PLANET MADE FROM POLYSTYRENE ROCKS AND A TEMPLE BOUGHT FROM HOMEBASE.'

'YOU MAY NOT ALL COME BACK ALIVE – SO GOOD LUCK BONES, SPOCK, SCOTTY AND, ERM, WILKINSON, ISN'T IT?'

'COME ON, CAPTAIN, WHEN DID WE LAST PUT PHASERS ON KILL?'

'HANG ON, WAS THAT A BRITISH POLICE BOX GOING IN THE OPPOSITE DIRECTION?'

'I KNOW IT'S A PARTY, CAPTAIN, BUT IT'S ILLOGICAL TO STICK CHEESE AND PINEAPPLE ON MY EARS.'

'WE'VE CURED EVERY KNOWN AILMENT IN THE TWENTY-FOURTH CENTURY, CAPTAIN PICARD — EXCEPT BALDNESS.'

'SLIPSHOD UNIFORM, UHURU. YOUR SKIRT IS ONE INCH BELOW YOUR FANNY.'

'SO, UHURU, THERE'S JUST THE TWO OF US LEFT TO PRESERVE THE HUMAN RACE — OH BOLLOCKS, HERE COME THE OTHERS.'

'I CAN'T GET A SIGNAL ON MY COMMUNICATOR — IT'S ON THE 3 NETWORK.'

'HELLO, MY NAME IS MICHAEL CAINE. MR ZULU — DON'T CHUCK THAT SPEAR AT ME.'

'WELL, IF THEY'RE TEASING YOU, MR SPOCK, YOU COULD ALWAYS PIN THEM BACK.'

# 14. UNLIKELY SMALL ADS

## FOR SALE

Is your penis too small? Call me, I have the world's smallest vagina.

Anything you want written on a grain of rice as long as it is one letter long. Failing that, anything you want written on a piece of paper.

I smell horrible. You can too. Call me NOW.

Learn to speak Mandarin in just 19 years.

Do you want me to come and burn down your house?

Become a paedo in one week with this easy-to-use kit. Includes beard, glasses, sandals and internet log-in.

Unwanted relatives hung, drawn and quartered in comfort of your own home. Call Steve.

Songs of The Beatles, as sung by my husband in the bath.

Organs harvested while you wait.

Learn to throw your voice and balls, I can't guarantee you both.

Me Tarzan, you Jane. Me mental, you not respond. Me get violent, you scared. Me need four male nurses hold me down.

Ex-Saddam lookalike seeks employment by new dictator who looks quite a lot like Saddam Hussein.

Send us £5 and receive as much as £4 back. If not completely satisfied then tough.

Amaze your friends. Win a Nobel Prize.

Beautiful women: come and make love to me, if not completely satisfied, your money back guaranteed.

Volunteers needed to be horrifically killed and buried in my garden. £5 an hour.

Want to make a noise like a dog? Call Frank.

Bushcraft and Survival Courses. Everything you need to know to survive in the most hostile natural environments. Every Monday, 7 p.m. Milton Keynes Leisure Centre.

I've overstretched myself. I've got a 12ft pole stuck up my arse. Buyer collects and yours for free.

Weird, unattractive pervert urgently seeking celebrity to stalk. Call now or just give me another signal through the telly

Sperm for Sale. Buyer 'collects' if you know what I mean.

Your nipples stretched or money back.

Tickets to Major Football Matches? Call ITV and ask for Robbie (Mum's the word).

Top quality, organic, fresh manure for sale. Buy Now. However, if you miss out, don't worry, I'll do another one tomorrow.

Students needed for risk-free clinical drugs trials; being desperate, impervious to pain and having no inquisitive relatives would be an advantage.

For Sale: State-of-the-art Home Cryogenics Centre, well OK, a freezer with a corpse in it for £20.

I am a really famous artist and desperately need beautiful women to come and pose naked in my studio for £20 an hour. Honest. Call Kev.

Cage Full of Young Tits For Sale: Blue, Great & 36 DD.

# 15. UNLIKELY PACKAGING (Part 1)

*Delia*
*Smith*
**DRESSING**
*Who wants to see that?*

*Cat's anus floating in bone-marrow jelly, covered in mouse droppings*

*Crispy bran flakes, ingredients: raisins, almonds, lethal levels of arsenic*

*Wholewheat bread, full fat cheese and 100% organic, corn-fed rat*

*Mozzarella, tomato, basil, mushrooms, snot, Dijonnaise mustard, rocket ... Hang on, did someone just say snot? Red onion, olives ... Snot? Are you sure? Peppers, cress ... Really? Snot? Yeah, it keeps the moistness, it's delicious, mmm, hummus, cabbage, you're fired*

*Rhubarb and Mustard ... oh dear, this looks like an unfortunate misprint to give to the company who prepared this*

*Deep-fried roadkill, might be a badger, could be a dog, at a push it might be a Polish roadworker*

*Toad in the Hole, ingredients: toad wrapped in bacon, drizzled in sauce, arranged so it looks like it's having penetrative sex with another dead toad. Yum!*

*Veal. Force-fed, container-transported, electric-prodded, bolt-killed and delicious!*

*Sherry-soaked sponge, custard, berry jelly, all topped off with a sprinkling of iron filings and asbestos*

*Arabian salad, ingredients: rocket, tomato, cucumber, feta, sheep's eyes (x2), camel testicle*

# 16. THINGS YOU DON'T WANT TO HEAR IN A PSYCHIATRIST'S OFFICE

'It's fairly obvious you have penis envy. I'll now put my trousers back on.'

'I'm worried about the results of your word association test – I've never had a patient say "murder" every time.'

'How long have you had these feelings of inferiority, you useless twat?'

'Before I treat you for your amnesia, could you pay the bill – and then, when we're finished, you can pay the bill.'

'Lie down and tell me about your phobia of couches.'

'You have a fear of paying extortionate bills? Well, I'd better sort that out, hadn't I?'

'I don't care if you do have multiple personalities – I can only see one of you at a time.'

'So tell me about your most harrowing sexual experience – only this time more slowly.'

'I'm happy to discuss your recurring feelings of guilt just as soon as you tell me where you're holding my family.'

'So, you're a depressive, drug addicted failure whose wife has left him and who is not allowed near his own children? OK, repeat after me: "Hakuna Matata".'

'Low self esteem? Are you familiar with the work of Freud? He paints lots of big fat mingers like you.'

'How ironic! Your penis looks just like Sigmund Freud.'

'Well having listened to what you have to say Mr Smith, I have to come to the conclusion that you are what we normally refer to, in the profession, as a complete c*nt.'

'I worry I'll never be capable of being faithful – as I was telling my other psychiatrist yesterday.'

'Well, I was hoping for a better diagnosis than, "You're a total nutcase."'

'I will only discuss the reasons why you think you're a monkey once you've stopped throwing your shit at me.'

'I'm going to regress you back to being a child of ten . . . now, tell me how I can upload pictures from my camera, to my computer?'

'Having heard the appalling details of your horrific childhood, might I recommend a couple of publishers?'

'I think I can trace all your problems back to you having a laughably tiny penis.'

'I keep seeing James Corden everywhere I look.'

'Never mind about your childhood.'

'Now tell me your most filthy dream and pass those tissues.'

'You lie on the couch and I'll climb on top.'

# 17. UNLIKELY THINGS TO READ IN A PARISH MAGAZINE (Part 2)

Parish Notices

Choirboy of the Month: Supple 13-year-old soprano Simon was very coy about being our April centrefold but we think you'll agree he's something worth making a song and dance about.

Fatwa of the Month: Mr Parkinson from number 18 for parking in a disabled space for two hours on Good Friday. Kill.

Childrens' Activities

6, 7, 8 June: Marbling, silk painting and printing (no booking necessary).

13, 14, 15 June: Smoking, daisy chaining and drinking (no booking necessary).

1, 2, 3 July: Tagging, happy slapping and cyber bullying (no booking necessary). Glue, alcopops and Meow Meow will be provided.

Please remember we are still conducting daytime Pilates on Monday mornings 11.45 a.m to 12.45 p.m. in the Community Suite. Please attend. If I have to sit here for one more bleak, lonely Monday morning scratching my arse and looking hopefully at the door, I'll fucking kill myself and it'll be all your fault.

The Townswomen's Guild meet on Saturday at 4 p.m. as usual. This week's speaker will be Nick Griffin.

Be Inspired! That's the theme of this month's magazine. Read it and vow to get the fuck out of this stifling, racist little hellhole.

LTA-registered tennis coach available for home visits offering high-quality tournament preparation for juniors and eight inches of stiff meat for their bored mothers.

The History Society meet in the Wibblethorpe Hall on Friday the 16th at 4 p.m., this month's speaker is Primrose Shipman who will be talking about 'Living with Doctor Death'.

**APOLOGY:** Last month's 'Musing' by the vicar should have read 'Peter had been fishing in a boat when he saw Jesus on the shore and jumped out', and not 'fisting'.

People often ask if I can explain the Parables. I can. They were stories some blokes in the old days made up to fill the Bible and try and make people think there was a God.

WANT COCK? MEET ME AT THE PHONE BOX IN THE SQUARE AT 3 P.M.

Spring is on its way; the primroses are poking out on the woodland edges and the green shoots of the bluebells are peeping through the carpet of fallen leaves. Peewits and Swifts cavort in the air and the local girls are getting into their summer dresses. I predict next week will be Tits Tuesday! First of the year! Wahey!

Film Club Church Hall

1 May *Driller Killer*

6 May *Last Tango in Paris*

12 May *Deep Throat*

# 18. UNPLEASANT CRISP FLAVOURS
## (Part 2)

**BOOM AND BUST**

**ROAST HUMAN SACRIFICE**

**SNAKES AND LADDERS**

**FOOT AND MOUTH**

**PEPPERED NAIL CLIPPINGS
AND DANDRUFF**

**VAG AND VINEGAR**

**MOUSE AND POISON**

**BILE AND SALIVA**

**ROHYPNOL AND PORK**

**PETROL**

**TRAMP AND CIDER**

**LIVER AND SPLEEN**

**SALT AND SMALLPOX**

**SUMP PUMP AND GARLIC**

**RABBIT AND DROPPINGS**

# 19. THINGS YOU WOULDN'T READ IN A CHILDREN'S BOOK (Part 1)

When the Squarepants came off, his mermaid bride realised why he was called Spongebob.

After one too many bangs on the head, Mr Bump suddenly flipped and went on a killing spree!

'You can call it a wardrobe, to me it's a closet,' said Peter, as he flounced into Narnia.

Unfortunately the Princess Rapunzel suffered from female alopecia and so the Prince plummeted to a horrible death.

See Spot walk. See Spot run. See Spot rub himself off against the corner of the sofa.

Mummy has herpes. Uncle Vince has herpes. Daddy has not got herpes.

'Any chance of seeing your secret garden, Hermione?' said Harry and Ron.

'Come on, Bunter!' said Bob Cherry. 'Take some Meow Meow like the rest of the sixth form!'

Cinderella had two ugly sisters – and one of them went out with Lembit Opik.

'These are "labia".'

Watch Spot die.

The wolf huffed and puffed – because he had an allergy to pigs.

As Prince Charming leant over Sleeping Beauty, he realised the Rohypnol had worked better than he'd hoped.

With ten seconds to go in the Quidditch final, Hermione hid the snitch in her snatch.

'Hello, Paul,' said Mary. 'What are you going to lubricate with that?'

Jenny has an apple in her pocket, Johnny has an apple in his pocket … oh no, that's not an apple.

See Spot turn malignant.

See my house. See my dog. See my penis. See the police knocking on my front door. See my futile attempt to erase my hard drive and escape out of the bathroom window.

How much is that doggy with a dildo?

# 20. UNLIKELY HEALTH AND SAFETY ADVICE (Part 2)

NOW WASH
YOUR BALLS

WORKERS ARE REMINDED TO PLEASE SHIT IN THE TOILET AND NOT ON MY DESK

CATCH IT, KILL IT, BIN IT AND THEN BURY UNDER PATIO INSTEAD IF BODY IS BEGINNING TO SMELL

OFFICE MORNING CHECKLIST: LOOK FOR SNIPERS AND BOOBY TRAPS; TEST FOR CHEMICAL AGENTS IN ATMOSPHERE; LOOK FOR SIGNS OF FORCED ENTRY BY HOMICIDAL INVADING ALIEN REPTILES. IF ALL CLEAR, PUT KETTLE ON, OPEN MAIL, CHECK ANSWER PHONE

THIS FACILITY IS FULL OF HAZARDOUS NUCLEAR WASTE. DO NOT EAT IT

ANYONE FLICKING ROLLED-UP BOGIES WILL BE FIRED ON THE SPOT

INHALING OTHER PEOPLE'S FARTS CAN CAUSE SERIOUS LUNG DAMAGE, IF YOU MUST BREAK WIND PLEASE GO TO THE DESIGNATED AREA BY THAT ANNOYING BRUMMIE BLOKE IN MARKETING

IN THE EVENT OF TOWERING INFERNO DO NOT ATTEMPT TO EVACUATE USING THE SCENIC ELEVATOR

THIS IS A HARD HAT AREA, IF YOU KNOW WHAT I MEAN

DANGER: PIERS MORGAN

ANYONE WHO SAYS 'ELF AND SAFETY' WILL BE SHOT

NOW WASH YOUR HANDS, ESPECIALLY IF YOU'VE JUST HAD A REALLY RUNNY SHIT AND YOUR FINGERS HAVE GONE THROUGH THE PAPER

IN THE EVENT OF FIRE, ADD RED ONIONS, MUSTARD AND CHILLI AND SERVE IMMEDIATELY

# 21. UNLIKELY THINGS TO READ ON THE BACK OF A BOOK (Part 2)

'I loved the sex scenes' – Gary Glitter

'Incredibly moving, the book of the year' – *Whizzer and Chips*

*The Aperçus of Richard Littlejohn: A Silva Rerum* is a delightful new compendium showing a new side to the celebrated polemicist. This joyful collection takes the form of letters, essays and a hilarious clutch of satirical Elizabethan madrigals addressed to his friends A. S. Byatt, Dr Jonathan Miller and his former partner Sir Dirk Bogarde. Lovely to see the real Dickie we all knew and loved at Oxford finally reveal himself.

Make your own filthy phone calls to minor celebrities with *The Russell Brand All-Star Phone Directory*, it's literally hilarious. 'Who would have thought Brian Cant lived in the 01296 area code?' – The Times. 'How did you get this number?' – Paul Shane from Hi de Hi. 'I'm afraid he's dead now, love' – the people who live in Don Estelle from *It Ain't Half Hot Mum*'s old house.

'In this exciting new volume, Harry Potter leaves Hogwarts and takes up a place studying Hotel Management at South Trent University'

'Easily Nick Hornby's best book' – Nick Hornby

'It's so nice to read a book that's on my intellectual level' – Wayne Rooney

'The best 50p I've ever spent'

£7.99

ISBN 978-1-84854-103-0

'This unauthorised biography of David Cameron had me almost gasping with excitement. But then I am a libel lawyer'

'The best novel about nineteenth-century crop rotation techniques written in the last three years'

'If you like this, you're gay'

'A brilliant read for people who are quite thick'

'Could do with a bit more shagging in it' – *Times Literary Supplement*

'I couldn't put it down' – Stephen Fry

'I couldn't pick it up' – Abu Hamza

'A pile of fucking shit' – The Most Rev. Rowan Williams, Archbishop of Canterbury

Dizzy PR whizz Lizzy Lovett is a fun 'n' feisty thirty-something singleton and Chardonnay-loving glitzy glamorous girl-about-town. Helped, and more often hindered, by her feisty 'n' fun flatmates, her hilarious search to find Mr Right before her biological clock stops ticking, is a marked departure for John le Carré.

''S alright, I s'pose, whatever' – A. S. Byatt

'£6.99 or nearest offer'

'Makes Dan Brown's books seem complicated'

'The cover is a nice colour' –
*Financial Times*

ISBN 978-1-84854-103-0

£7.99

## 22. UNLIKELY THINGS TO HEAR IN A COURTROOM

'I do not recognise this court – you've had it painted since I was here last.'

'If I may object to my learned friend's point using, err … coitus interruptus, camera obscura, I mean curriculum vitae cunnilingus.'

'Clear the courtroom! The defendant has just farted.'

'Summon the bloke who did it – I mean "the accused"…'

'It is my belief you took this very dagger and plunged it into the hapless victim again and again, like so … oops!'

'Silence in court! – I'm trying to listen to the cricket.'

'Foreman of the jury, have you reached a verdict?' 'Not yet, m'lud, we feel we need another free night in the luxury hotel.'

'What do you mean "contempt of court", you jug-eared twat?'

'If you think you can get off by pleading insanity, you must be mad! … Ah.'

'Mr Michael Mouse – you stand before me accused of buggery, how do you plead?'

'All be upstanding … and when the music stops, the last one left still standing up is out.'

'See my testimony? Sorry, I thought you said testicles.'

'You will be taken from this place to a dark room where you will be tickled with sticks until you wet your pants.'

'Can I stand like this so the court artist can get my best side, please?'

'We find the defendant guilty as a girl can be, of love in the first degree.'

'Not guilty! Great. Does that mean I can keep all the money?'

'Please don't finish cross-examining me yet, this is my only acting work so far this year and I've not had a chance to show my full vocal range.'

'Good evening, Your Honour, here are the results of the French jury: Royaume Unis guilty, la Turquie not guilty.'

'Wig! Wig! Wig!'

# 23. WORRYING EMAIL SUBJECT LINES

**Inbox — Folders on My Computer**

Inbox    Calendar    To Do List    Sent Directly to Me

Folders on My C...
- Inbox
- Drafts
- Outbox
- Sent Items
- Deleted Items
- Junk E-mail
- Microsoft News ...
- Microsoft News ...
- Mail Views

**Inbox** — Filter

**Yesterday**

Re: Your impending death

Re: Last night – I'm really a man

Could you look at this picture of one of my poos?

Re: Incriminating pictures of you

Re: Gun trained at your head

Re: The poison you ate last night

I've given you chlamydia

Re: Shadow on your lung update

I think you sexually assaulted me last night

Re: Getting my car back out of your kitchen

Greetings from your accountant in my new house in Buenos Aires

That was your last warning

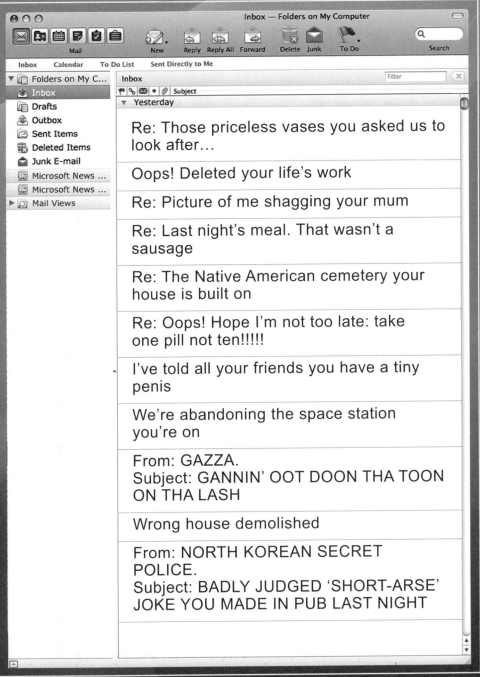

# 24. UNLIKELY TITLES FOR MEMOIRS (Part 1)

TERRY V BRIDGE: WHO WAS BETTER? *by* Vanessa Perroncel

MY LIFE AS A TRANSVESTITE *by* William Hague

YOU'RE ALL C*NTS: FUCK YOU *by* Julie Andrews

THE FAT ONE WAS SHIT *by* Syd Little

I WAS HERE ALL ALONG *by* Lord Lucan

YES, IT IS A WIG *by* Terry Wogan

OUR LOVE *by* Ant and Dec

OUR LITTLE SECRET *by* the Pope

MORE THAN JUST A PAIR OF TITS *by* Miranda 'The Tits' Melons

A LAUGH, A SMILE AND A SONG *by* Robert Mugabe

BIGGER THAN THATCHER, BETTER THAN CHURCHILL
*by* Iain Duncan Smith

MY LIFE APART FROM ALL THE TENNIS STUFF
*by* Tim Henman

NOT JUST A KILLER *by* Peter Sutcliffe

# 25. BAD THINGS TO SAY ON YOUR FIRST DAY AT WORK (Part 1)

'I've been mashed off my face all week, but I should be able to fly the plane OK.'

'Is this how we put the holes in the doughnuts?'

'I'm pregnant, when can I start my maternity leave?'

'Well, it's a tricky one, isn't it? I mean, define "paedophile".'

'This is my desk. Why do they call you Mad Mary?'

'Sorry, I thought dress-down Friday meant I had to come in naked.'

'Just let me check, you want the tigers in the cage or out of the cage?'

'So, who's the office bike, then?'

'Hello, Sir Alan, I can't come into work, I'm ill.'

'Photocopies of my arse, anyone?'

'I'm guessing it's you who makes the coffee round here, love.'

'I've just seen your stationery cupboard, and it's like an Aladdin's cave in there.'

'Where can I put my collection of musical gonks?'

'Hey, the reason I put your packed lunch in the shredder is because it's funny.'

'Do any of you postal workers know where I can store my rifle?'

'Hi, I'm Coco, the new clown. I expect I have some big shoes to fill.'

'Why do they call this stretch of the sewage system "curry corner"?'

'Can I use piss instead of embalming fluid?'

'It's the first Monday in the month – why am I the only person who's blacked up?'

# 26. UNLIKELY LETTERS TO A RIGHT WING TABLOID

Sir,
Could we have more stories about immigration, house prices and people swearing on TV please?

Sir,
Do the BBC really think it is right to see two male characters kissing passionately in a soap opera before the watershed? I have no wish to see their taut, firm bodies quivering as the surge of pleasure jolts through them, their manly yet sensitive hands given licence to rove all over each other, their moist lips … sorry, I need to lie down and … be punished.

Sir,
Some of your stuff is a bit strong, isn't it? Yours, M. Ahmadinejad

Sir,
I have just watched the BBC programme *In the Night Garden* and was shocked to see the character Upsy Daisy brazenly kissing several of the other characters and objects. This promotion of promiscuity is a sign of how out of touch the filth-mongering grossly overpaid lefty-loonies at the British Brainwashing Con-peration are, I blame the disgusting grossly overpaid, untalented Ross.

Sir,
Where was the Princess Diana article today? Surely you can't have us believe that thirteen years after her death there were no relevant stories concerning her.

Sir,
I was going to write you a letter but my computer just started typing gibberish. It's a PC gone mad.

*Sir,*
I have recently moved here from a foreign country. How has this been allowed to happen? I blame the soft-touch new government. Please have me deported before I can't help myself and start sponging off the State.

*Sir,*
I was disgusted to see swearing on BBC2 at 9 p.m. last night and there was some dancing and speaking in tongues and a woman had a poppet with a needle, she's a witch, burn her...

*Sir,*
Piss poo wank tits gypsies gays the BBC Jonathan Ross immigrants lefty PC.

*Sir,*
What has happened to the Nigel Dempster column? I miss finding out how an earl who was briefly famous in 1962 and minor European royals are getting on.

*Sir,*
I'm foreign, gay and really enjoy using a rolled-up copy of your newspaper in my depraved sex acts that are too hideous to describe in a family newspaper. Try and stop me! Xxx

*Sir,*
Thank you for your recent valuable articles about things that can give you cancer. I am now living solely on Rich Tea biscuits and cranberry juice in a hermetically sealed box.

*Sir,*
I have lost track; am I a national treasure or an evil, money-squandering homosexual this week? Love, Elton John

*Sir,*
How come Fred Bassett hasn't died? He must be over forty years old by now. What do you feed him on?

*Sir,*
Thanks for all your support and a Merry Christmas to all your readers. Yours, A. Hitler

# 27. UNLIKELY THINGS TO READ ON A MOTORWAY SIGN

Picnic area and shallow grave site

Hugely disappointing theme park – 2 miles

Jessica. Call Me. Please

Speeding amnesty ahead. Fill your boots

Last dogging site for 112 miles

Beware: people driving like c*nts ahead

Blackburn Ahead. Beware 4,000 holes

Have you now or at any time been involved in genocide?

1950s gangster walled up in bridge ahead

Don't read this sign, you'll crash

Turn on fog lights – there is no fog

Sinister hitchhikers next five miles

How's my immigrant smuggling?

Caution: You have left the gas on

# 28. UNLIKELY BOARD-GAME INSTRUCTIONS (Part 2)

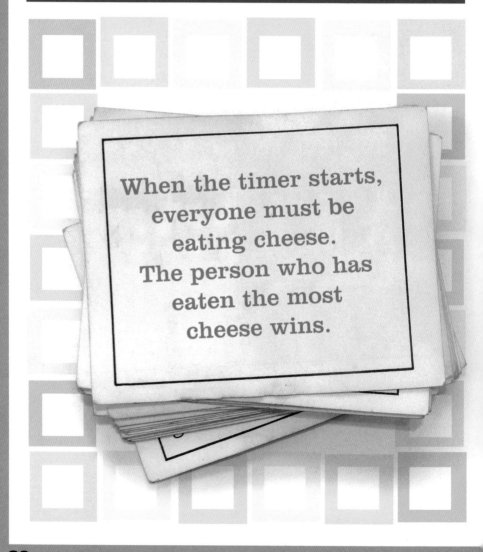

When the timer starts, everyone must be eating cheese. The person who has eaten the most cheese wins.

Raise a lot of money, go out to sea, find a wreck, bring the treasure to the surface. The person with the highest value haul starts.

Compare penis lengths. The person with the longest starts.

If you roll two ones on your first go, you must scream 'FUCK!' at the top of your voice until ejected from the house.

Whoever rolls the lowest must be shot.

*Treasures of the Sahara*. In this box you will find all you need to play: sun screen, £200,000, provisions for fifty days and a Bedouin guide.

Shakespeare's female characters were inevitably stronger and more impressive than his male leads. Discuss.

Press the button and the cage with the hole will begin to revolve, goad the lion until the cage stops and whoever is sitting in front of the hole when it stops will be toyed with, brutally savaged and then eaten.

Take seven tiles. Spell out the rudest word possible. When someone spells MINGE, the game ends.

Everyone has a card and a claw hammer. If two matching cards are placed down on the board, hit the person to your left with a claw hammer.

Remove the scorpion with care and drop it down the top of another player of your choice. During the intervening struggle, all other players should read through the Resuscitation Booklet and the first to successfully revive the victim is the winner.

# 29. UNLIKELY PHRASES TO FIND IN A PHRASEBOOK
## (Part 1)

UTTER

'Have you found your legs? They are in the sea.'

'Where are my nipples?'

'I think you may be full of shit.'

'Am I able to polish my artichoke in your building this evening?'

'What the fuck are you staring at?'

'I want £10,000 in unmarked bank notes or your wife gets it.'

'Would it be possible to see your breasts, please?'

'Your Prime Minister cannot win his election as his policies are malfunctioning.'

'Do I need planning permission for this erection?'

'I would like to have a hold of your ham.'

'Yes, but can you bottle them?'

'May I now remove my hand from your testicles, please?'

'Jesus, Maureen. Will you put on some make-up?'

'My dog has bled to death in your kitchen.'

'My urethra has been invaded, can you help ease the pain?'

'Could you direct me to Hereward the Wake?'

'Is this a cheese-free zone?'

'How much are your children?'

'My pancreas is rumbling.'

'Here, take my inside leg away and measure it.'

'Pooh, what a terrible smell, is that you?'

'Hello. You seem like a right c\*\*t.'

# 30. THINGS YOU WON'T HEAR ON A GARDENING PROGRAMME

' ... making it an ideal height to have a piss behind.'

'It's a small, quite ugly plant with a noxious odour, sort of the Paul Daniels of the plant world.'

'And if you want to bury a relative in a shallow grave, September is probably the best month and this is a good way to do it.'

'And you bring the shovel down on the mole's head like this, repeatedly.'

'A flower bed is like your wife, it needs to be cared for, nurtured, solidly laid and covered in excrement.'

'And you insert the tip of the gnome's hat like so...'

'And over there, just behind the vegetable patch, I've got a lovely convenient branch of Tesco Metro.'

'It's two parts liquid compost, one part weedkiller – that's what I call a drink!'

'So, pack your fertiliser in tightly, and you're just about ready to blow up Parliament.'

'There it is – a steady stream of liquid manure – but I don't write the scripts.'

'Every shed should have everything a gardener needs for a good day's work. Trowel, secateurs and a collection of dog-eared old porn mags.'

'This is a bit boring, I know, but later in the programme Rachel de Thame will be bending over.'

'To get rid of slugs some people use pellets, but I prefer to use live ammunition.'

'These bamboos grow at six inches a day – wow, that's more than my dick!'

'The pea flowers will wrap themselves round these wooden pegs, so let's just bang one in and ... arrggh shit, shit, shit.'

'So pruning these in September will mean an amazing bloom in May and, oh, who fucking cares, I wanted to present Newsnight.'

'This compost heap will smoulder for hours but if you want to guarantee a flame, throw some dead cows on.'

'Over here I've planted some blue flowers, and here's some red stuff and these are those ones like my mum used to have.'

'This is mint, this is rosemary, and over here in the concealed greenhouse is the strongest shit north of Morocco.'

'For this week's project we're going to dig up Percy Thrower and use him as organic fertiliser; it's what he would have wanted.'

'And this flower's got a very distinctive smell. It's just like ... well ... spunk, isn't it?'

'Here's a tip for anyone trying to grow tomatoes. Just buy them from the supermarket, you big hippy.'

'When you offered to show me your collection of hoes, Mr Diddy ...'

# 31. UNLIKELY HEALTH AND SAFETY ADVICE (Part 3)

THESE BEARS
MAY BE
ENDANGERED –
BUT THERE'S NO
LAW AGAINST
GOADING THEM
WITH A STICK

DO NOT OPERATE THIS MACHINE WITHOUT ARMS

DO NOT BREATHE IN OR OUT WHILST IN THIS ROOM

DO NOT PUT SUPERGLUE ON YOUR PENIS... AGAIN

IF ANYTHING SHOULD BE SPAT ONTO THE GROUND, DO NOT ATTEMPT TO EAT IT

PLEASE TAKE CARE WHEN PREPARING FOOD DUE TO BACTERIA; IT'S EVERYWHERE, EVERYWHERE DO YOU HEAR ME? WHY WILL NO ONE LISTEN? WHEN ARE WE GOING TO DO SOMETHING? THEY'LL KILL US ALL! LISTEN TO ME

CHOKING HAZARD: RUSSELL BRAND'S COCK

CONSULT YOUR DOCTOR BEFORE OPENING THIS DOOR

IF YOU FART, YOU MUST REPORT IT TO THE NEAREST DESIGNATED HEALTH AND SAFETY OFFICER IMMEDIATELY

WARNING. SHIT

DO NOT OPERATE THIS MACHINE IF YOU ARE OR EVER HAVE BEEN A HOMOSEXUAL

TRACHEOTOMIES MUST NOT BE PERFORMED WITHOUT PRIOR MEDICAL TRAINING

DON'T LAUGH AT THE NOISE THIS MACHINE MAKES

RADIOACTIVE PROTECTIVE CLOTHING MUST BE WORN AT ALL TIMES APART FROM LUNCH OR IF HAVING A SHIT

FOR THE PROTECTION OF OTHER EMPLOYEES PLEASE FIND ANOTHER JOB

NOW FUCK OFF

# 32. THINGS YOU DON'T WANT TO HEAR ON A SPACE FLIGHT TO MARS

'Are we there yet? Are we there yet? Are we there yet? Are we there yet?'

'This Easyjet space shuttle to Mars will soon be landing on Neptune, where a bus will take you the rest of the way.'

'It can't be that hard to fly this thing, it's not rocket science.'

'I don't want to worry anyone but the pilot has switched off the computer and intends to rely on the Force.'

'Our excursion to the Sun has had to be postponed because it's night time.'

'We are now in the gravitational pull of that fat woman's arse in Row C.'

'We will be reaching Mars in nine months and we apologise to passengers in economy whose entertainment systems don't work.'

'Welcome aboard this exploratory space mission to create an equal and entirely free society. Passengers in First Class can now enjoy lunch.'

'Hey amazing, watch what happens if I don't use the bag to pee in.'

'Hey, what happens if I unscrew this?'

'I think maybe when I was getting the frozen fish I might have switched off the human life support systems.'

'I'm your pilot, Major Tom, and I'm just getting in contact with Ground Control.'

'Hello, I'm Michael McIntyre and welcome to my Space Roadshow.'

'I'm a bit nervous about this five-year flight to Mars, do you mind if I whistle?'

'This is your captain speaking. Don't worry about being scared of flying, it's only natural, I'm shitting myself.'

'Oh, we've had the map upside down.'

'I spy with my little eye something beginning with S. Space? No. Star, yes.'

'Don't worry about anything, you're in safe hands ... ten, nine, seven, er, eight, five ...'

'The temperature at the centre of the Sun is 93 million degrees, so don't forget to wear a hat.'

# 33. THINGS YOU WON'T HEAR ON A HISTORY PROGRAMME

'And from that moment on, King Edward the Second bitterly regretted saying to his servant, "For all the good you're doing with that red-hot poker, you might as well shove it up my arse."'

'Seventy years ago, Germany invaded Poland, in a move that would be unthinkable today. Well, I say that – but if I were Polish, I'd be watching my back.'

'Many a Scottish sailor was saved from scurvy by the introduction of the deep-fried lemon.'

'It was on these very cave walls that Stone Age man first drew a big hairy mammoth . . . cock and balls.'

'Tonight on Five, the history documentary that TV commissioners have dreamed of: *Did Hitler Sink the Titanic?*'

'Before she got her famous lamp, Florence Nightingale would always be banging her head on things – hence her original nickname, the Lady with the Lump.'

'In building the Pyramids, how did the Egyptians move so many huge blocks of stone? Two things: slaves, and whips.'

'Now, as a replacement to the advertised programme *French Weaving in the Eighteenth Century*, which clearly wasn't going to get us any viewers, we're now showing *Basic Instinct*.'

'In tonight's programme *Roundheads versus Cavaliers* find out if the staunch Puritan troops are any match for a fleet of flamboyant Vauxhall cars from the 1970s.'

'I'm going to cut a small trench eight inches deep. I'm busting for a dump and the toilet's miles away.'

'And now an in-depth look at the reign of King Charles Eleven. I mean King Charles the Second – sorry, it's my first day.'

'While Rome burned, Nero fiddled – then put down the child and played his violin.'

'If you want to learn more about Native Americans you can go to www dot – or, as they might put it, "woo woo woo!" dot . . .'

'This mummified head has been on Bruce Forsyth's body for more than eighty years.'

'Before he entered the pyramid, Howard Carter stopped to relieve himself. This became known as "The Riddle of the Sands".'

'Goebbels and Goering – did Hitler ever muddle them up?'

'The historical significance of the Tudors is enormous, but all you need to know is that you will be getting to see Anne Boleyn's tits.'

'Disappointingly, the metal detectors have only picked up the broken metal detectors we left here last year.'

'It was here that the most powerful Queen of all was born: Peter Mandelson.'

'And the team in Trench 1 are having problems. They're being fired at by the German archaeologists in the opposite trench.'

# 34. UNLIKELY PACKAGING (Part 2)

PORK PIE
(THIS IS AN INSTRUCTION RATHER THAN A DESCRIPTION)

*May contain nuts, but then again, it may not. Who's to say?*

*Mixed biros, contents: two red, two blue, two not working*

*Yorkshire pudding – contains E-by-gum numbers*

*Carcass Wellington, slowly decomposing corpse of a dead animal wrapped in pastry and ready to serve*

*Vomit and mushroom pie. It's a pie with mushrooms so disgusting, when you eat them you'll immediately vomit back into the dish*

*Greek salad, ingredients: tomatoes, feta cheese, olives, tzatziki. NB: can also be used to aid anal penetration*

*Andrex toilet paper – strong enough to strangle a puppy, but not so strong you won't poke a finger through*

*Tennis racket – serves two*

*Shove up arse before going through customs*

*Hot apple pie, ingredients: molten lava and pastry*

*Sausages – 100% pork (trotters, snout and lips)*

*Serving suggestion – don't bother*

*5 Loaves and 2 Fishes. Feeds 5,000*

*Caution: This babushka doll may contain other babushka dolls*

*Shit salad, ingredients: rocket, tomatoes, lettuce, red onion. And shit*

# 35. THINGS THAT WOULD CHANGE THE ATMOSPHERE AT A DINNER PARTY

'Erm … I don't want to worry anyone, but I've just seen the Statue of Liberty's head bouncing down the street.'

'Your wife has very good taste in clothes. I've just been through her underwear drawer.'

'I won't smoke, thanks – the gelignite in my pants is quite unstable.'

'Now I can never remember – is it beer before heroin or the other way round?'

'Well, I think the Khmer Rouge had a point.'

'I've never seen cheese and pineapple sticks on a real hedgehog before.'

'Oh – it's a "Vicars and Tarts" party. Sorry, Reverend – and your daughter.'

'That looks just like my Louis XIV bureau on that bonfire.'

'Oh sorry, is this not a naturist event then?'

'John! You were supposed to try and get the orange under her chin, not up there!'

'OK, so this is me with the golden eagle I shot.'

'The funny thing is if I hadn't overslept it would have been me flying that plane into the Twin Towers.'

# 36. HARRY POTTER TITLES YOU'LL NEVER SEE (Part 1)

*Harry Potter and the Donkey's Genitals*

*Harry Potter and the Wheel of Cheese*

*Harry Potter and the Haliborange*

*Harry Potter and the Bucket of Shit*

*Harry Potter and the Rack of Lamb*

*Harry Potter and the Half-Mast Pants*

*Harry Potter and the Cock of Fire*

*Harry Potter and the Bag of Tea*

*Harry Potter and the Kiss Me Quick Hat*

*Harry Potter and the Confit of Duck*

*Harry Potter and the Application of Sudocrem*

*Harry Potter and the Wonky Supermarket Trolley*

*Harry Potter and the Ring of Onion*

*Harry Potter and the Goblet of Jizz*

# 37. LINES YOU WON'T HEAR IN *STAR TREK*
## (Part 2)

'THIS IS THE ENTERPRISE LAVATORY WHERE EVERYBODY BOLDLY GOES. AND YES, THAT IS THE CAPTAIN'S LOG.'

'SPOCK, YOU POINTY EARED C'NT.'

'CAPTAIN, WE HAVE VISITED THE FUTURE WHERE YOU ARE IN A CRAP TV COP SHOW AND HAVE RELEASED SEVERAL EMBARRASSING ALBUMS.'

'SO NOW YOU TELL US, BONES, YOU'RE A DOCTOR OF MUSIC.'

'CAPTAIN KIRK, THERE'S A STRANGE LIFE FORM ATTACHED TO THE TOP OF YOUR HEAD — MY MISTAKE, IT'S A WIG.'

'OH NO, WE'VE BEEN FLASHED AT WARP FACTOR FIVE, THAT'S EIGHTY QUID DOWN THE PAN.'

'OK, NEW REGULATIONS, BEFORE I BEAM YOU DOWN YOU HAVE TO HAND OVER ANY LIQUIDS OVER 100 ML.'

'TAKE THE BRIDGE, SPOCK, I'M GOING ON THE TUBE. RACE YOU.'

'CAPTAIN'S LOG. STAR DATE 28.19. WHAT KIND OF STUPID SYSTEM IS THIS? ALRIGHT, IT'S THE 14TH OF OCTOBER.'

'SHIT, I'VE ACCIDENTALLY BEAMED THE TRANSPORTER DOWN TO ANOTHER PLANET.'

'DAMN, MY PHASER IS INCURRING HUGE ROAMING CHARGES ON THIS PLANET'S NETWORK.'

'DR McCOY, YOU'RE BEING STRUCK OFF FOR NOT NOTICING SPOCK'S EAR TUMOURS.'

'CAPTAIN'S LOG. STAR DATE 23.69. TODAY I DECIDED TO ORGANISE A DRESS-DOWN FRIDAY.'

'CAPTAIN'S BLOG. STAR DATE 23.87. HERE'S A LINK TO AN AMUSING CLIP OF A CAT PLAYING A PIANO.'

'BAD NEWS, CAPTAIN. OUR MISSION IS BEING UNDERCUT BY A NEW VESSEL: EASY ENTERPRISE.'

'SPOCK, IS THAT A VULCAN DEATH WANK?'

'SPOCK, I NOTICE FROM THE TIGHTNESS OF YOUR TROUSERS THAT VULCANS HAVE THREE TESTICLES.'

'I'M AFRAID DR McCOY IS OUT PLAYING SPACE GOLF.'

'DON'T SHOOT, IT'S THE PIZZA DELIVERY BOY.'

'IT'S THE NIGHTMARE SCENARIO, CAPTAIN. THE EVENTUALITY WE HOPED WOULD NEVER HAPPEN HAS HAPPENED. THERE REALLY ARE KLINGONS ON URANUS.'

# 38. UNLIKELY THINGS TO HEAR ON *CRIMEWATCH*

'It was then that the police approached Crimewatch, and asked us to help them project a large bat-shape onto the clouds.'

'Police are baffled. They are stuck on 3 Down on the Sun's coffee-time crossword.'

'String the fuckers up. It's the only language they understand.'

'The gang are believed to be tough, but fair, and they only ever murder people what have transgressed the unwritten code. They love their old mums and frankly we should leave them to sort out the scum.'

'Here's an artist's impression of the suspects. Unfortunately, the artist is Tracey Emin – and she's represented them in the form of a collection of tents with the word "Suspect" embroidered on them.'

'Don't have nightmares, although, don't forget that my former co-presenter was motivelessly murdered on her own doorstep in broad daylight.'

'Police have issued this photofit of someone they'd very much like to talk to. It's Jessica Alba.'

'Don't have nightmares – but do check under the bed, just in case.'

'I'm afraid this week's edition of Crimewatch has been cancelled, as someone has nicked all the cameras.'

'There is a sizeable reward on offer. Unfortunately, it's from the Lotto Rapist and it's for keeping your mouth shut.'

'Here's an artist's impression of the suspect – he must be guilty, look how close together his eyes are.'

'Well, we did have one caller and I'm anxious to talk to her again as we seemed to have quite a lot in common.'

'Each of these fake pound coins costs approximately one pound to make, and has a street value of one pound.'

'Police have named the man who's been terrifying unsuspecting members of the public – it's me.'

'Remember, don't have nightmares. Ooh, this news just in – the Midnight Strangler has just escaped, and is on the loose. Goodnight.'

'If you were in the area, watch closely and see if it jogs your memory. If not, just sit back and revel in some poor bastard's misfortune.'

'How many people saw this arse sticking out of this car on the M1 at 12.30 last night? No one? Thank God for that.'

'Put that back you slag. I seen you, put it back! Understand?'

'Have you seen this man? He may be of Greek or German origin but speaks with a posh English accent, lives in a palace and is in the habit of shooting rare birds.'

'The police are looking for a man with a small black moustache who may have invaded Poland in 1939.'

# 39. THINGS YOU DON'T WANT TO HEAR FROM YOUR FLATMATE

*I HAD TO BORROW A CONDOM BECAUSE YOUR mum and SISTER CAME ROUND*

—X—

'I've cleaned the toilet – oh, and your electric toothbrush needs recharging.'

'It's not the sleepwalking per se that's a problem, it's my incontinence.'

'From next week Sharia law comes into effect.'

'Next time you and your girlfriend have sex, could you get her to face the wardrobe?'

'I'm sorry, but we're leaving Mum's coffin in the living room.'

'You said I could bring Tweety Pie with me – you never asked me if it was a pit bull.'

'I'm sorry, I can only sleep with the light on – in every room.'

'I don't think we should flush after every dump, do you?'

'I'll take the room at the back – the one that overlooks the playground.'

'I've moved the fridge into your bedroom – I like to snack while I'm watching you sleep.'

'That's the washing-up done – I don't think I've ever licked so many plates.'

'I know you don't like me having a dump when you're in the shower, but I've mashed most of it down the plughole.'

'He might be a tramp but he's my tramp, and I love him.'

'Guess what? Ever since my cat got that urinary tract infection he's found your pillow really comforting.'

'Fancy a girlie night in with duvets, Special Brew and some animal porn?'

'I'm just putting the chainsaw on again, it helps me get off to sleep.'

'I've done a thorough spring clean – I've finally tipped out your vase full of dust, the one labelled "Mum".'

'Can you come and wipe my bottom?'

'Now there's a coincidence ... I met him last night on Hampstead Heath and turns out he's your dad.'

'Ta-da! Now you go and put on *my* clothes!'

'Someone phoned last night ... something about being left money in a will ... but you must respond within twenty-four hours ... didn't write it down.'

'Don't have a go at me for using your towel – you're the one who forgot to buy toilet paper.'

# 40. BAD THINGS TO SAY ON A FIRST DATE (Part 1)

'Nag, nag, nag – don't you ever shut up?'

'Order whatever you like – though, from the look of you, I'd stick to the salad.'

'I've brought along my mother for the evening.'

'Sorry I'm late, I've just come from an honour killing.'

'How do you do? Now if you'll just wait, I have to describe you on Twitter.'

'Hello (puts finger in ear). OK, she's here. Now what do I say?'

'You smell nice – like chip fat.'

'I'll order for three – our Saviour is always with us.'

'Will you marry me? Please? You're my last chance. I'm desperate.'

'Would you like to see the long-distance photos I've taken of you?'

'Now why don't you pop to the bathroom and make yourself look nice.'

'Don't mind my scratching – it's just anal scabs.'

'Yes, I have been on TV – but I don't like to talk about it. I was on *Crimewatch*.'

'Yes, and it's not just Greek *food* I like.'

'Please take note, when it comes to paying the bill, I'm not having a starter or a coffee.'

'I hope you enjoyed yourself tonight – because, thanks to my lifetime pass, I can take you back to Spearmint Rhino as often as you want.'

'OK, I admit I did choose a photo for the website that didn't show my conjoined twin.'

'I'm just going to the bathroom to freshen up – oh, and have a massive shit – so you order.'

# 41. UNLIKELY PHRASES TO FIND IN A PHRASEBOOK
## (Part 2)

UTTEF

'It isn't going to suck itself, your Highness.'

'Officer, someone appears to have taken my kidney.'

'I tire of your flippancy in this country. Now you must die.'

'I think you will find that my sister is very affordable.'

'Would you mind helping me rub down my ox with a rag?'

'Can I briefly put my ring road through here?'

'You have no interest for me at all, can I please now have my vest back?'

'Excuse me, but I couldn't help wanking to what you were saying just now.'

'Schnell! Schnell! Teufel Hunden! Gott in Himmel! You win zis time, Tommy!'

UTTERLY USELESS PHRASES

'I have circumnavigated the market and believe you are not as heterosexual as your mother would have us believe.'

'Five minutes is what I would give that if I were you, Penelope.'

'Arrgh. I must have been fingered on the Tube. It had to have happened when I was paying for my ticket.'

'Christ! That's huge! I could never take that.'

'I appear to have had a sexual experience in the wrong tent, officer.'

'I am the Emperor of the Universe, but you can call me Al.'

'£10 for that? Surely you are indulging in an amusing subterfuge.'

'Give me the Elgin Marbles back, you twats.'

'Could you direct me to the nearest sewer, please?'

'I am shitting through the eye of the beholder.'

'Crouch down and help me find my suppositories.'

# 42. UNLIKELY TITLES FOR MEMOIRS (Part 2)

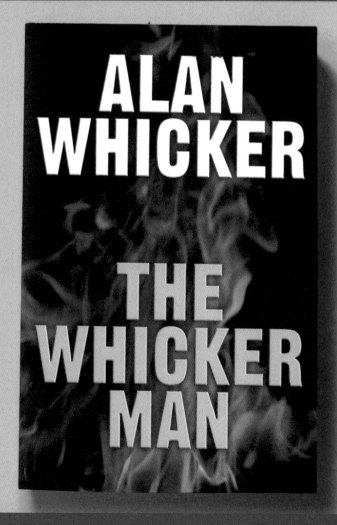

ALAN WHICKER

THE WHICKER MAN

SCENES WE'D LIKE TO SEE

I WON'T BE AS POPULAR WHEN YOU READ THIS *by* Vince Cable

THANK HEAVENS FOR LITTLE GIRLS *by* Gary Glitter

GIVING HEAD IN A LAY-BY AND OTHER STORIES
*by* Gillian Taylforth

EYE TO VAGINA: THE BERNIE ECCLESTONE STORY

CANED AND ABLE *by* Max Mosley

HOWERD'S END *by* Frankie Howerd

DON'T HAVE NIGHTMARES *by* Jill Dando

GO WEST *by* Rose West

18 HOLES *by* Tiger Woods

ONE FOOT IN THE GRAVE *by* Michael Foot

GOOD EVENING, HERE IS THE HUWS *by* Huw Edwards

TURN YOUR HEAD AND COUGH *by* Dr Josef Mengele

JESUS H. CHRIST! THE AUTOBIOGRAPHY OF GOD'S ONLY SON

# 43. LINES YOU WON'T HEAR ON A TV TALENT/ VARIETY SHOW

'So, Amanda – what did you make of Les Dennis's rendition of "Don't Leave Me This Way?"'

'Three hundred years ago you'd have had to bribe a jailer to see this.'

'You've won … two months in the Priory!'

'This final could go either way – it's either the poof or the stammerer.'

'Turns out the guy who sawed the woman in half wasn't a magician, he was a psychopath.'

'You could be the best mentally ill singer this country's ever had.'

'You're too old, you can't sing, you're clearly just desperate to be on TV – please welcome back Amanda Holden!'

'I would put you through, but I'm not sure whether training a dog to do that is actually legal.'

'Simon, I am an alternative sword-swallower. I shove them up my arse.'

'Thanks to a body-piercing accident, I shall perform a tribute to James Galway using only my penis.'

'I know it's not been done before, but sawing a dove in half wasn't really that entertaining.'

'Prince Philip is going to the Royal Variety Show this year so that's why the finalists are three strippers, two racist comedians, a self-mutilating gimp and a man who tortures badgers.'

'Say hello to Mr Phallus, children.'

'I shall now attempt to juggle THREE apples.'

'So does your dog do anything else other than shit on the stage?'

'So to send a middle-aged woman into rehab call this number, or alternatively to make a six-year-old burst into tears on live telly, call this one ...'

'That may count as a talent down in deepest Somerset, but I'm afraid the Metropolitan Police would like a word with you afterwards. And your chicken.'

'When you said you were a Gary Glitter tribute act, we weren't expecting you to do that ...'

'Here's a little character you'll love: "Golliwog the Cannibal". Say hello everyone, he's very shy.'

'Ladies and gents: the Formation Prostitutes of Amsterdam.'

'So I then burn the asbestos like so ...'

'If you're as good a mind-reader as I think you are, you'll already know you were shit.'

'Welcome to the show where we look for the best finalists who are either talented, mental or grieving.'

'Knife throwing – yes. At the audience – no.'

'That was a superb Elvis impression – the way you sat on the toilet trying to shit while eating a burger.'

'Grapefruit was an interesting choice. I've only ever seen that performed with ping-pong balls.'

# 44. BAD NAMES FOR NEW CHOCOLATE BARS (Part 1)

*Cadbury's Trauma*

*Weasel*

*Caramel Corpse*

*Chocolate Haemorrhoids*

*Cripple*

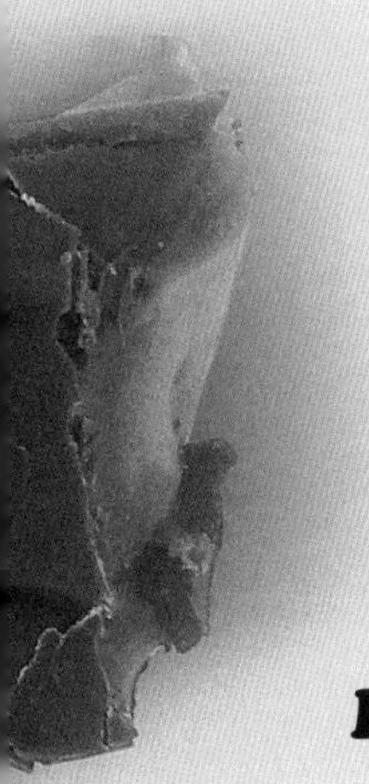

Ripper

Meow Meow

Taliban

Slut

Chocolate Droppings

Adenosine Monophosphate

Dairy Cheese

Swamp Gas

Dairy Diarrhoea

Walnut Wank

Ebola

Vadge Slime

Hershey's Dirty Protests

Uranus

# 45. BAD THINGS TO HEAR AT CHRISTMAS

'No, Dad, it's "Wink" murder.'

'It is a big present, isn't it, Granny? It's your own headstone.'

'We need a new sofa and a carpet – if only we knew where there was a sale on.'

'Santa couldn't bring you a toy train – so he's brought you a toy replacement bus service instead.'

'Call the plumber, dear – I'm off for my Boxing Day dump.'

'I thought being an atheist you wouldn't want anything.'

'If he's anything like me he'll enjoy playing with the box – so we got him the box.'

'What's this? Eurgh – someone's come down the chimney.'

'Ssh! Everyone – it's time for Colonel Gadaffi's Christmas Speech.'

'When I asked for a chipolata with my Christmas turkey, Mr Berlusconi, I was not inviting you to dip your cock in my gravy.'

'Noel Edmonds is on all the channels at once. He must be jamming the signal.'

'Mr. Scrooge? I am the Ghost of Suspect Year End Tax Returns.'

'Right, who wants to play a game? I'll get a biscuit, you all undo your trousers.'

'I had a sneaky look at your laptop, so I know you'll like hardcore animal porn.'

'And now, Britain's most lovable heroes cook up a new moneymaking scheme in *Wallace and Gromit and the Illegal Dogfighting Ring*.'

'Ah, it's just what I always wanted! Your mother's choked to death on a date.'

'Don't be silly, children, the Wii belongs to you, not Granny. Oh, I see what you mean.'

'It's better to give than to receive – but if you do like receiving, meet me here at these toilets tomorrow night.'

'Is that all you wanted this year, son – a new dog, some KY jelly and some bangers?'

'Remember, don't have nightmares, but I imagine Christmas Eve is a bloody likely time to get burgled.'

'How thoughtful – a secondhand butt plug.'

# 46. UNLIKELY JUNK MAIL (Part 1)

You are currently six feet from a rat, please pass on this urgent message from his mum.

Buy 1 pizza – pay full price.

Manure dumped at your house tomorrow, ring this number if not convenient.

The takeaway curry you ate last week has been recalled.

Dear No. 31, we've tarmac-ed your drive and tiled your roof. Sorry. We thought you were No. 13.

Time wasted, while you wait.

We'll be in your area tomorrow collecting unwanted toddlers, love Madonna.

Enjoy the taste of India – dysentery, disease and open sewers.

Garden rubbish cleared, into next door's garden. If not interested, please pass leaflet to a next-door neighbour.

Have you seen my dog? I do hope not, because he does a massive dump on your doorstep every morning.

Have you seen my pussy? No? Well, come round and I'll give you a look.

No more waiting ... heart, lung, liver surgery done in the comfort of your own home. Also odd jobs.
Contact 'Dr Mick' on this number.

Can you find better typesetters than us? Bet you c*nt.

# 47. BAD THINGS TO SAY ON YOUR FIRST DAY AT WORK (Part 2)

'Does anyone want to see my cock ring?'

'Just because I'm the new boy in the mortuary, I'm not having anyone's sloppy seconds.'

'If I can't touch the children, what's the point of working here?'

'Oh, you said prick his boil.'

'I suppose the perk of working down the sewers is you can take a toilet break any time?'

'It's an easy mistake to make – I had no idea I was meant to be here as a pheasant plucker.'

'I trust none of the lads on the building site will have a problem with me being gay.'

'Where's the company nurse? I've got a really itchy cock.'

'I know it's only Monday but I thought I'd dress down today – I don't think I'll still be here on Friday.'

'Help me out, nurse – which one's the hip bone connected to?'

'Ten minutes early, but I like to have a really big shit before I start cooking.'

'But I've always had a picture of a Thai ladyboy for a screen saver.'

'Is there a busy shopping centre nearby where I can start randomly shooting at people?'

'I know it's not nice to vomit, but at least I got it in the bin.'

'I wasn't wanking, I was rubbing in some aftersun.'

'Sorry, but you shouldn't keep the insulin next to the Domestos.'

# 48. UNLIKELY PACKAGING (Part 3)

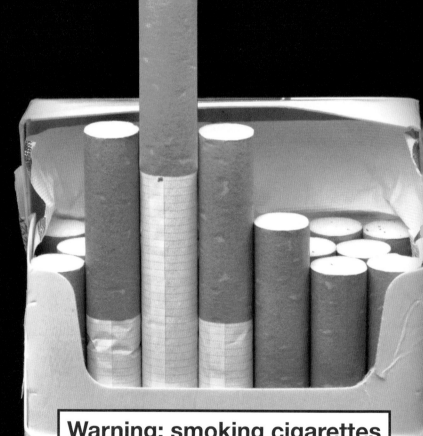

Warning: smoking cigarettes may cause tutting

*Safety matches, average contents: 45 matches. Like you're going to check*

*Frosted flakes: contains free model of terminally obese child*

*Eton mess, ingredients: ginger biscuit topped with lashings of freshly squeezed first-form semen*

*Contains one mozzarella and smoked-salmon flavoured condom*

*Fish fingers: contains last ever cod*

*Self-assembly shelves: packet contains everything needed to assemble, except for one vital small metal strut*

*Luxury crisps, contents: largely air*

*This backpack may contain clothes, or a bomb. You decide*

*Gordon Ramsay's Fucking Cream of Fucking Tomato Soup. It's fucking delicious*

*Contains riboflavin - whatever that is*

*Serving suggestion - come in from pub and pour straight into mouth*

*Contents: half a pound of tuppeny rice, half a pound of treacle. Warning - may cause weasels to pop*

*Alphabet soup - may contain N, U, T and S*

# 49. UNLIKELY FIRST LINES OF LOVE SONGS

'One day I'll show my love for you, but at the moment it feels like I'm pissing razors.'

'You seem like the most beautiful girl in the world, but I can't see much from where I'm hiding.'

'You were made for me ... out of plastic.'

'Come on Eileen, there's come on Eileen.'

'If I said you had a beautiful body would you let me wipe my cock on your curtains?'

'You've got beautiful blue eyes. I'd like to pickle them in a jar.'

'I like Piña Coladas and getting caught in the rain. Well, I drank eight of them and fell asleep in the garden.'

'My love for you is growing ... well, my penis is getting bigger.'

'Your beauty is priceless, but I could go to £100 for an hour.'

'Your love for me hurts so much, you might have to try putting it in the front bottom.'

'I love you more than the rotting corpse of my mother up in the loft.'

'Love me, love my dog ... but not in exactly the same way.'

'You make my heart beat faster every time you come near me, but that's mainly because I'm hiding in your cupboard.'

# 50. UNLIKELY THINGS TO HEAR A SAT NAV SAY

'Are we there yet?'

'Hang on - I've got the map upside down.'

'To escape the Child Catcher, drive off approaching cliff, deploy brightly coloured red and yellow wings and launch into upbeat musical number.'

'Just drive and don't ask any questions.'

'If possible do a U-turn. I think you left the gas on.'

'Now we're alone together there's something I need to tell you.'

'What do you mean how do I get to Halfords, you're not buying a new Sat Nav, are you?''

'Well, now we're going to be late, are you happy?'

'I'm sorry. I don't have this river on my databasglub. Glub. Glub.'

'I'm leaving you for a better driver - someone who listens!'

# 51. UNLIKELY BOARD-GAME INSTRUCTIONS (Part 3)

New Kersplosh!
Everybody takes it in turns
to shit in a bucket of water.
Whoever makes the
biggest splash wins!

Everybody squeezes the pig, the person who makes it squeal the longest is then arrested.

You are now ready to make an accusation, e.g. 'It's bound to be the black guy in the car park with a spanner.'

Place the biscuit in the centre of the board and all begin masturbating.

Person who rolls lowest is the victim, everyone then takes it turns to punch or kick them until consciousness is lost.

If you roll a six on your first go, then you're a c**t.

Once they have taken the Rohypnol, begin handing out the tokens.

When the timer starts you have 60 seconds to piss yourself.

Once you've received your arms, invade another country using tactics of shock and awe.

Deal the cards in a deceitful manner to ensure you will win.

Each player needs four cards and a blow torch.

Whenever a six is rolled, the player dons the plastic glove and completes as many rectal examinations as possible until the next six is rolled.

Whoever lands on the Green Square is deemed to be 'The Grass' and must be tarred, feathered and lashed using the materials provided. They must also miss a turn.

# 52. BAD THINGS TO HEAR IN HOSPITAL

'Can you feel that? You can feel my finger? Do you like it? Does it feel good? Yeah? Shit, the doctor's here.'

'I think I might be in the wrong hospital; the man in the bed next to me is Ian Brady.'

'I'm afraid we've cut your cock off by mistake, but all the nursing staff tell me it was really small anyway.'

'I'm afraid your normal gynaecologist is away. Would you mind if the YTS lad had a look?'

'Good news about your breast implants, we were doing three for the price of two.'

'Clear! Oh bollocks, the battery's flat.'

'Now the CAT scan does show up something in your stomach. Tell me, have you landed on any distant planets and had a squid thing attached to your face recently?'

'Do you want to take the bone home for the dog?'

Beeeeeeeeeeeeeeeeeeeeeeeeeeeeeeeeeeeeeeeeeeeeeeeeeeeeeeep!

'I need 40cc's of adrenalin, nurse. Its been a really long shift and I've got this complex operation to do.'

'Pass the bone saw. Now – did you mean my left or the patient's left?'

'So your notes say you're the very serious Mrs A? Oh hang on – MRSA, sorry.'

'The good news is, your new knee joint is working perfectly. The bad news is the surgeon didn't realise you were lying on your front.'

'Mr Nick Griffin? I'm Dr Omgugu from Nigeria, and I'll be treating your haemorrhoids today …'

'Nurse, what's the bleeding time?'
'I don't fucking know.'

'Scalpel, scissors, your lovely tight arse …'

'The screaming? That's the drug trials down the corridor.'

'We don't use local anaesthetic any more, just take a swig of this, bite down on the wood and try not to listen to the saw.'

'I'm not surprised you threw up your steak and kidney pie, a body often rejects other people's organs.'

'We've X-rayed your throat now and it appears the blockage was a massive cock.'

'You'll be in this ward with the big mute Indian chief and Nurse Ratched.'

'Now we don't want to alarm you, but this is your solicitor, your immediate family and Father O'Flannery.'

'I realise you're trying to make this anal probe as easy as possible, Doctor, but do we need the mood lighting and music?'

'If you can't make it to the toilet, just pull the cord and one of the nurses will come and humiliate you while you shit the bed.'

'Here is a pellet – just swallow it if anything goes wrong during the operation and you get caught.'

'See? I told you it was the left one.'

# 53. UNLIKELY TITLES FOR MEMOIRS (Part 3)

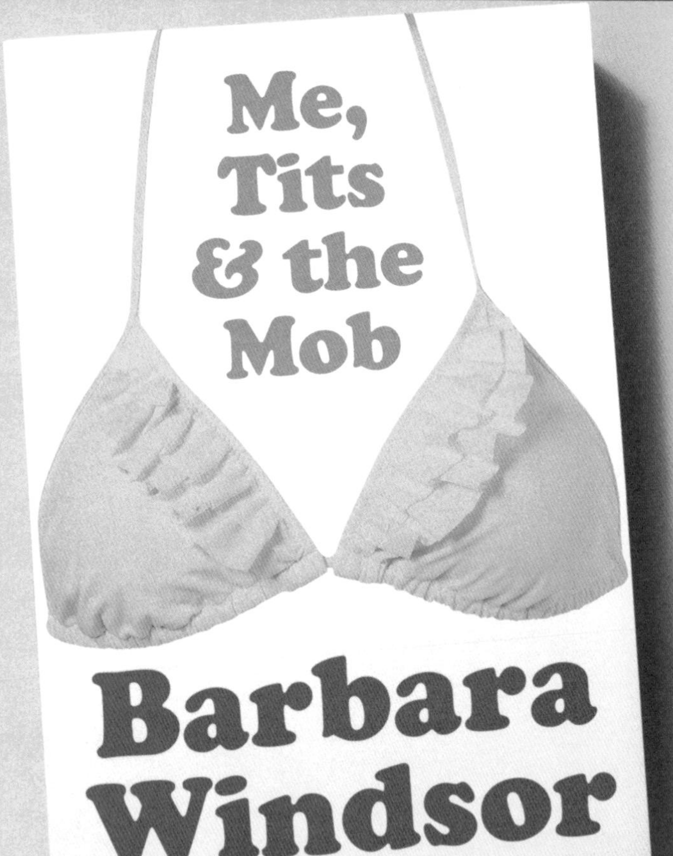

Me,
Tits
& the
Mob

Barbara
Windsor

TAKING A STAB *by* Steve Irwin

THE FUCKING UNITED: THE ALEX FERGUSON STORY

SHIT! SHIT! MY HEAD'S ON FIRE *by* Niki Lauda

A WHOLE POT OF TROUBLE: THE AUTOBIOGRAPHY OF POL POT

A KICK IN THE GULAGS *by* Joseph Stalin

FAIR ENOUGH, IT WAS CLEARLY AN ACCIDENT
*by* Mohammed al Fayed

THE WORTHLESSNESS OF FAME *by* David Beckham

NEVER MIND THE RENT BOY *by* Mark Oaten

SEX, DRUGS AND ROCK 'N' ROLL:
THE TRUE STORY OF MY CAREER IN POLITICS
*by* Gordon Brown

HITLER: MY PART IN HIS DOWNFALL *by* Winston Churchill

MEDITATIONS ON THE NATURE OF SPORT AND SOCIETY
*by* Wayne Rooney

SALADS, SMOOTHIES AND GYM CIRCUITS:
ON TOUR WITH PETE DOHERTY

# 54. UNLIKELY THINGS TO HEAR ON A DIY SHOW

'This old room has high ceilings, a draughty fireplace and 1930s wallpaper. So we're going to leave it alone – it's got a lot of character.'

'So, with a housebrick in each hand like so, you're now ready to neuter the dog.'

'This 1960s bungalow needs some careful renovation and months of work. But we've only got a week, so we're just going to bugger it up and leave it.'

'We've made the kitchen much more light and airy, by taking the roof off and then running out of money.'

'Down go the floorboards, then the underlay and the carpet, nail it down, and believe me, no one is going to find that body for quite some time.'

'So that's how you plumb a toilet, now sit back and relax and watch me take a dump. Goodnight. Hrrrrruuurrgh.'

'Well, that's the whole back wall of the house down. Shit. I'm off before the owners get back.'

'And then simply use the nailgun, or hammer them hard to the plank. If that's what gets you sexually excited, good luck.'

'This shelf above me is going to be there for years – OW!'

'Welcome to Total Wipeout DIY. It's the Total Wipeout that we know and love, only carrying a working chainsaw and a hair-trigger nailgun.'

'I find lead-based paint is best for a child's bedroom.'

'And remember, the size of the letterbox you want to fit is dependent on how large a turd the local kids will be shoving through.'

'And remember, the motto for all DIY jobs is "Fuck it, that'll do".'

'I find I don't need a tool belt, I just bend over and stick the spanners down the crack in my arse.'

'If you haven't got a nailgun, I'd recommend bodging it with some glue.'

'Tonight on *Tricks of the Trade* we'll be trying to get rid of that massive dump I had last night in the toilet.'

'So that's how you knock two rooms into one. So here we are in one small room with a really, really high ceiling.'

'If you drop a chainsaw, never, ever try to catch it. Isn't that right, Stumpy?'

'Now, on the subject of decking – who wants to punch Nick Knowles first?'

'There we are, another perfectly ordinary house shoddily transformed into a tart's boudoir.'

# 55. UNLIKELY AD SLOGANS

*Softer and longer than your grandfather's cock*

*Rosehip fresh – really hides that smell of shit*

*Leaves you with a feeling of immense regret*

*Does exactly what it says in the Bible*

*A shave so close that you'll bleed*

*That's fresh, arsehole fresh*

Precision engineering by some German c*nts

*Now with new botulism*

*Incontinence pads – at last I can have a piss on a crowded tube*

*For those stubborn stains: you know, shit, blood or
when you've accidentally wanked onto a shirt*

*Melts in your mouth and then corrodes your intestines*

*Will probably give you cancer*

*Kills pain fast but sadly also kills you within 24 hours*

*Your headache will stop instantly but then your
arse will bleed uncontrollably*

*Are you paying too much for your hit man?*

*The most fun you'll have without wanking*

*9 out of 10 dogs prefer Chum, but that's
not saying much, is it? I mean, they'd scoff a
dead pigeon covered in shit if you put it in front
of them, let's be honest*

# 56. BAD THINGS TO SAY TO A POLICEMAN (Part 1)

'I thought you had to be above a certain height.'

'What does a Taser feel like then?'

'Do you mind if I do this to your horse with my finger?'

'Never mind me – you were going faster.'

'Are you going to arrest my cock for impersonating a policeman?'

'You'll never take me alive, copper!'

'I wanted to be a policeman when I was little, and then I passed some exams.'

'You already have a sample of my DNA, all over your mum's tits.'

'What do I win if I manage to knock your helmet off with these balls?'

'You know, I've only just realised how gay riot gear looks.'

**POLICE LINE** **DO NOT CROSS**

'You'll never find the drugs – I hid them in a very private place.'

'Oi, Filth. Race you to the next set of lights.'

'No – you turn out your pockets.'

'Let me go, and the rest of this McSandwich is yours.'

'Thank God you're here, officer – I've lost my trousers somewhere on the heath.'

'Can you settle an argument for us – do these joints we're smoking count as class B or C?'

'Handcuffs? Kinky.'

'Are you going to take down my particulars, big boy?'

'Why not make me get out of the car?'

POLICE LINE                    DO NOT CR

# 57. UNLIKELY DICTIONARY DEFINITIONS (Part 2)

**Hamlet** (*pr.*): type of cigar. Shakespeare stole the name for use in one of his crappy plays.

**hand** (*n.*): unit of equine measurement. This is the only meaning of the word 'hand'.

**Lampard** (*pr.*): any form of fat cheating Chelsea bastard, he dived, it was never a penalty and he ruined my accumulator.

**last** (*adj.*): not first, as in *Last of the Summer Wine*, *Last of the Mohicans*. Where I used to finish in every school sports race, but I'm over that now.

**lunch** (*n.*): something that changes everything, as the song says, 'Lunch changes everything'.

**maneuver** (*v.*): I can never remember how to spell this, so it might be in the wrong place and you might have to 'manoeuvre' it back. Geddit? Sorry.

**olives** (*n., pl.*): I don't like these, especially black ones that haven't been stoned. Just to reiterate, I am just talking about olives, OK?

**pissflap** (*n.*): you know what it is, let's not be coy about this, do you feel dirty?

**pissflaps** (*n., pl.*): totally different to above, just wanted to do it again.

**pob-pob** (*n.*): word my fourteen-month-old son uses for his toy train. Hopefully it'll catch on.

**quango** (*n.*): a type of fizzy drink. This might not be right actually, is it a thing in politics? Yeah that's it, quango: thing you read about in papers and stuff.

**shat** (*v.*): past tense of shit, e.g. 'Hey everyone, I've just shat myself. Look.' 'Sorry everyone, I appear to have shat myself. I couldn't help it. Oh dear.' (Shak) 'Romeo Romeo, I heard you coming and shat myself.'(Kafka) 'As Gregor Samsa awoke one morning, he found he had shat himself.' (Wordsworth) 'I wandered lonely as a cloud because I had shat myself and stank.'

**smegma** (*n.*): sorry, I'm not discussing this, you've only looked this up to get me to say it. This is not appropriate.

**snot** (*n.*): stuff that comes out of your nose, as in 'Look at all that snot coming out of your nose.'

**tits** (*n., pl.*): wahey!

**Um Bongo** (*n.*): popular exotic drink native to Congolese people.

**wank** (*n.*): I'm having one now, actually.

**waste** (*v.*): as in squander, ruin, basically what I have done with my fucking life.

**water** (*n.*): something to drink when there's nothing else or when you are trying to show your key worker that you've changed.

**willy** (*n.*): slang for penis, as in 'Do you mind if I stick my willy in your foo-foo?'

**xuqghzlf** (*adj.*): word I have to put into the dictionary as I used it to score 715 and win a game of Scrabble last Christmas. It's a type of old tool or something, yeah?

# 58. BAD THINGS TO SAY ON A FIRST DATE (Part 2)

'Vodka always turns me into a randy lecherous beast. Waiter! Two vodkas, please.'

'Do you mind if I write about this in my Dating Disasters column?'

'Let's just split everything tonight, including the condom.'

'I've never met anyone like you before, but then I have been in solitary confinement since birth.'

'OK, cards on the table ... that's me, busty Barbara DD, new in town – I usually just leave it in a phone box.'

'Sorry, I've just realised I must be a homosexual.'

'I'm different from other girls – I've got a penis.'

'Women I've had sex with? Is that counting Mother or not?'

'Anyway, you're droning on ...'

'That drink taste normal, does it?'

'So I thought – back to mine for some coffee and anal sex?'

'We'd better skip dessert – the hotel room's only booked for an hour.'

'So, do *you* think I killed Jill Dando?'

'I've got this terrible spot on my forehead ... can you squeeze it for me?'

'You've got beautiful eyes, and your cleavage has given me a boner.'

'Before I order the food – if I'm not happy after a week, I can send you back to Thailand, yeah?'

'Have you met Emu? Say hello, Emu!'

'I thought we'd check out the museum of torture, then dinner, then finish at an S&M club before returning to my constituency.'

# 59. UNLIKELY JUNK MAIL (Part 2)

BRITISH BUILDERS PRETENDING TO BE POLISH

Ying Tang Chinese Restaurant grand reopening after salmonella outbreak.

Raj Indian Restaurant. Curries so hot your shit will literally be steaming.

Can I come and live in your house? Thanks.

Want to speak French? Well, maybe you should have worked harder at school when you had the chance.

Banana for sale. Act soon before offer ends.

Have you seen my lost dog? No? Not surprising, your windows are so bad I'm amazed you can see anything! Call Dave's Windows on this number.

Farm Fresh Milk. From the farm this morning. They won't even have noticed it's missing yet.

My name is Magda, I can clean and babysits for your childrens. Or more if your wife away.

Pizza Delivery. Only £8.74. None of our drivers carry change.

Noisy Scaffolders Ltd. Large metal poles thrown off lorries at 6.30 a.m. prompt.

Leery Builders are in your area. Ask about our sexual harassment rates.

We've just opened a new Poor Pun Hairdressers in your area.

Recession Pizza Company. It's like a meal out, only not at all.

Jehovah's Witnesses. We called, but you pretended not to be in.

# 60. UNLIKELY THINGS TO HEAR ON A PA SYSTEM (Part 1)

'Will the owner of the car with the registration "C O O L D U D E" please be aware that he is a massive twat.'

'Will the (crackle) in the (crackle) come and fix the (crackle) PA system.'

'The 16.24 will be leaving at 16.25, a fraction over twenty-four hours late.'

'If anyone's lost a small boy he's been found on platforms 13, 14 and 15.'

'The train will be delayed because of short staff – we're trying to get a cushion for the driver.'

'We're going to be held in this station for a while because London Underground is shit.'

'David Beckham will be book signing for the next two hours, after that he's going to try and write his name in a second one.'

'Welcome to the Star Trek convention. There will be a raffle later, where first prize is a life.'

'Would the owner of the BMW penis extension please return to the car park.'

'We have an eight-year-old boy called Michael who has made his way to the Information Desk. Any paedophiles who wish to meet an eight-year-old called Michael, please make your way to the Information Desk.'

'Clean-up in aisle six; pornographic magazines.'

'This is your Captain speaking. If you look to your right you can see Detroit and if you look to your left you can see a man with his underpants on fire.'

'Doors to manual and cross check … does anybody know what that means?'

'Coach C is a Quiet Carriage because everyone in there is … dead. Ha! Ha!'

'This is your driver speaking. That signal we just passed, was it red or green?'

'We will shortly be arriving in Penzance – sadly this is the 4.33 to Edinburgh.'

'We apologise for the delay – this is due to the fact that we're shit.'

'This is your Captain speaking. I have put the fasten seatbelt sign on as I'm banging the stewardess and we don't want to be disturbed.'

'Hang on – should I try and remember to take all my personal belongings with me when I leave the train? If only there was some sort of announcement to help me!'

'We are sorry for the late running of this train, which is caused by a signal failure at make somewhere up.'

'The 1810 will now be leaving, two hundred years late.'

Because of Sunday engineering works we're being re-routed via Islamabad.'

'Tickets please. Heil Hitler!'

# 61. ILL-ADVISED PAINT CHART

Irritable Bowel
Syndrome

Cub Scout on a
Rollercoaster

STD Piss

Holiday Rep's Liver

David Dickinson

Tube Driver's
Hanky

Dodgy Barbecue

Swollen Testicle

Old Dog Poo

Daily Mail Reader's Face
After Being Wished
'Happy Winterval'

British Army
Economy
Camouflage Suit

Cerise (Is that like
sort of reddy? I can
never remember?)

Worrying shit

Goth's Bottom

Boris Johnson's
Pubes

Wanker's Bowtie

Seasick

Newborn's Nappy

Berlusconi's Hair

# 62. UNLIKELY THINGS TO HEAR ON *ANTIQUES ROADSHOW*

'This is a marvellous – ungh – collection – ungh – of nineteenth-century erotica – ungh – that's me finished.'

'I've examined the painting closely – 1799 is the price, not the date.'

'I thought this might interest you – it's Hugh Scully's skull.'

'This is a lovely item – we don't have many copies of the Bible actually signed by Jesus coming up for auction.'

'They're much too stumpy to be Queen Anne legs – they're more Duchess of York.'

'This is an astonishingly rare item – a copy of the *Express* with no mention of Diana, Madeleine or house prices.'

'Yes, this was actually mine and it was stolen earlier this afternoon.'

'Ah yes, a house, these were very popular at one time but basically worthless now.'

'(Unzips trousers) Well, how much is it worth to you?'

'The date here reads 1665, year of the Great Plague and – look out, I'm going to throw up.'

'There is quite a collectors' market for antique magazines, but the fact that the centre pages are stuck together will reduce its price, as will the fact that it seems to have been kept in a hedge.'

'I'd say this chamber pot dates back to Victorian times – though the turd is definitely more recent.'

'Yes, the image of Jesus, there, clearly visible on the slice of toast. Worth absolutely nothing, you mentalist.'

'And this priceless Ming vase … WHOOPS, er, Ming puzzle …'

'This would appear to be the very jacket Lord Nelson wore at Trafalgar – which you've nicked from the National Maritime Museum.'

'As to the value, I'd estimate this as worth about thirty quid – although the crestfallen look on your face is priceless.'

'I know it's technically an antique, but a bottle of vanilla essence three years past its sell-by date isn't what we're looking for.'

'I don't think Fiona Bruce will care to look at that – and if you don't put it away I'll call the police.'

'This specimen is over two hundred years old and still presenting *Strictly Come Dancing*.'

'Let's have a look at what you've got … why, it's a worthless bit of shit. Next!'

'I don't think this can be a genuine Rembrandt because, as far as I know, Rembrandt didn't paint Dogs Playing Snooker.'

'This car is quite valuable. You can tell from the tooth embedded in the steering wheel that it once belonged to Richard Hammond.'

'This antique commode has some writing on the side. Here we are, it says, "Are you looking for cock?"'

# 63. UNLIKELY LINES TO HEAR IN A HORROR FILM (Part 1)

'Igor, I've always wanted to ask you this. I'm a seven-foot monster; couldn't you have given me a bigger dick?'

'I didn't like the look of the old log cabin, so I've booked us into a Travelodge.'

'Oh no - when I experimented with the transportation device there was a fly in with me - on a dog turd.'

'I've used spare body parts I retrieved from corpses and put a bolt through his neck. With these NHS cutbacks that's the best I can do.'

'Can you face the flames, the blood, and the craving for raw flesh? If so, come to my barbecue next Sunday.'

'In the dawn of a deserted London inhabited only by zombies, one man searches desperately for a night bus.'

'There's a murderer on the loose? I'd better strip off and have a shower.'

'I'm sorry, there's a convention on - the Bates Motel is completely full.'

'Surely if you're a ghost you can go anywhere. Why are you hanging round this dump? Why aren't you on a beach somewhere?'

'She's vomited up some green slime - but then this is Ayia Napa.'

'Yes, I'm a werewolf - I'd like a back, sack and crack please.'

'Apparently he knows what I did last summer: worked at a food factory and then went InterRailing, well he could have got that from my Facebook account.'

'I looked in the mirror and said, "Handyman handyman handyman," and he still didn't show up to finish my kitchen.'

'I'm going into the cellar now. Fucking hell! There's a pool table down here, fantastic.'

'Good news: I wasn't giving birth to an alien. Bad news: it was last night's curry.'

'Oh my God, look around you, no famous actors, this is either a porn film or a horror movie.'

# 64. BAD THINGS TO SAY TO A POLICEMAN (Part 2)

'You have got the biggest breasts I've ever seen on a middle-aged man.'

'When are the Red Indian and the construction worker coming?'

'Thank God you've arrived, a man has climbed into my boot and shot himself fourteen times.'

'Do you ever feel stupid in that hat?'

'How did you keep up with me? I was doing 182 miles an hour.'

'What's the matter? Doughnut shop shut early?'

'You can look everywhere, except the boot.'

'Hitler Youth full up, was it?'

'Sorry, officer, but was that a 5p that just fell out of your pocket? Perhaps we can forget the whole thing?'

POLICE LINE DO NOT CROSS

'Can we reenact those car chases from *Smokey and the Bandit?*'

'Yes, I have been drinking, officer. Or I wouldn't be brave enough to call you a fat-faced bastard.'

'Is that a truncheon in your pocket or are you just pleas ... oh, it's a truncheon.'

'Two of you, one of me ... I make that Pimms o'clock.'

'Those handcuffs don't fit me ... your wife and I have established that.'

'Blue really brings out your eyes.'

'OK, let's do it the hard way.'

'Keep back – I'm carrying a table leg.'

'It's up my arse, want a look?'

POLICE LINE          DO NOT CR

# 65. UNLIKELY HEALTH AND SAFETY ADVICE (Part 4)

BEWARE: CONTENTS HOT. DO NOT POUR ON GENITALIA

DON'T BE A C**T

BEFORE ENTERING THESE PREMISES, WIPE ARSE THOROUGHLY

WHILST UNDER THE INFLUENCE OF THIS MEDICATION, DO NOT OPERATE HEAVY WOMEN

HAVE FUN, CHILL OUT. GO MAD. YEAH

THERE MUST BE NO DANCING, NO USE OF POPPETS, NO WITCHCRAFT. ANYONE WHO DISOBEYS WILL BE BURNED. BY STRICT ORDER GOODY PROCTOR AND THE REVEREND HALE

DON'T MAKE ME COME IN THERE

STAND UP IF YOU HATE MAN U

DO NOT LIE DOWN IN FRONT OF TRAINS

DANGER: EROTIC DANCERS AHEAD. BEWARE FLYING PING-PONG BALLS

BEFORE ENTERING THESE PREMISES, ABANDON HOPE ALL YE

BEFORE GOING UPSTAIRS, THINK, 'DO I REALLY NEED TO GO UPSTAIRS?'

IF TAKEN ILL, NOTIFY FIRST AIDER AND HOPEFULLY THEY'LL CALL SOMEONE WHO KNOWS WHAT THE FUCK TO DO

IT IS AN OFFENCE TO WEAR GREY WITH GREEN. ESPECIALLY WITH YOUR HIPS, LOVE

BEFORE ENTERING THE ROOM, CHECK YOUR FINGERS DON'T SMELL

# 66. UNLIKELY AWARD CATEGORIES

'The British C**t Awards. Categories include: Most Annoying C**t in a Light Entertainment Programme, Most Promising New C**t, Biggest C**t in a Foreign Language, the overall prize for C**t of the Year and a special Lifetime Fellowship of the C**t award.'

'The PUFTAs, incorporating Closet Homosexual of the Year.'

'Crufts Turd of the Year, Best Humping of a Leg, Most Flamboyant Licking of Testicles, Arse on Grass Rub Challenge (you know that thing they do), Most Disgusting Thing Eaten, Most Expensive Thing Chewed, Toddler Savaging of the Year, Most Questionable Relationship with Owner, Lifetime Arse Sniffer, Least Impressive Trick, Tastiest (this applies to the Korean event only), the Spot Least Imaginative Name of the Year.'

'The British Fart Awards. Smelliest, Loudest, Longest Lasting, Most Inappropriate, Longest Held In, Silentest and Deadliest, Illest, Wettest, Best in a Foreign Country, Best Avoiding of Blame Award, Most Enclosed Space.'

'The Grit Awards: Britain's finest gritting companies, hosted by Ray Stubbs and Lesley Judd.'

'Catholic Paedophile of the Year Award, live from Dublin.'

'Most Unamusing Title.'

# 67. UNLIKELY THINGS TO HEAR AT AN AWARDS CEREMONY (Part 1)

'Lindsay Lohan for Best "Actress" Who Never Actually Appears in Any Films.'

'And the winner is … nobody in this category. You were all shit.'

'And Rear of the Year goes to: half of Vanessa Feltz.'

'Now to the award for Best Foreign Film. This is the award, oh, what's the point they'll only edit this one out.'

'I'll just open the envelope, and announce that … my STD test has come back positive.'

'And in a hilarious mix-up, the Children's BAFTA goes to *The Devil's Whore*.'

'And the nominees for Thinnest, Poshest and Most Annoying British Actress are: Keira Knightley, Thandie Newton, Sienna Miller and Kate Beckinsale.'

'The award for best actress goes to Catherine Zeta-Jones for saying "I love you" to Michael Douglas on a regular basis.'

'We'll take an ad break now while all the stars nip off to the loos to cane some charlie.'

# 68. THINGS YOU WON'T HEAR FROM A GOLF COMMENTATOR

'Oh no, the ball's landed on the grass and now it's going to drop into that little hole, they'll never get it out of there!'

'And I think Els said, "If you miss this, you're gay."'

'And he gets out his wood, in the rough. He must need a piss.'

'Brilliant, two men walking about with a bag full of sticks on a horrible day in the north of Scotland.'

'He hits it through the clown's mouth, up the dragon and into the castle...'

'A disappointing eighteen holes – the moths have been at my Pringle sweater.'

'That's a bogie – but he's wiped it on his trousers.'

'I don't know about you but I can't wait for the fucking football season to start.'

'A fascinating anecdote there from Peter Alliss.'

'He's asking the caddy to reach in and give him six inches, frankly you'd think they'd wait until he'd handed in his score card.'

'Woods waits over his tee while those three blokes from Bradford & Bingley hack their way out of the bunker.'

'Ha ha! It's hit a spectator on the head!'

'He's had quite a day, he's shot three birdies, two eagles and an albatross. Someone must explain to Prince Philip that isn't the idea.'

'Oh no, he's ended up in the wrong hole ... and not for the first time, if what I've heard...'

'It's landed on the M25, he's going to have to play it from the central reservation.'

'Look at that ball, high and white in the air against a leaden sky, no idea where it is or how good it is from this angle.'

'Sorry, I'll be honest – I nodded off there.'

'Apparently there's a golf sale in town, but I couldn't find a sign for it anywhere.'

'With those check trousers and tasselled shoes he looks every inch a twat.'

'Tiger Woods drops another shot against the unexpected tournament leader, Ronnie Corbett.'

'Here comes Tiger Woods ... shouldn't be allowed really, but what can you say.'

'A succession of long chips for Colin Montgomerie, followed by a bit of fish and a pickled egg.'

# 69. UNLIKELY IN-FLIGHT DUTY-FREE ITEMS

This **secret masturbation kit** includes fake arm and hand, pocket hole-cutter and 'Hey look, I'm sleeping!' mask.
Price: £24.99

**Vomit in a Spill-Proof Cup**. Just add water and you have a cup full of vomit. Like magic!
Price: £6.99

Steal info from the person next to you with this easy to use **wi-fi bugging device**.
Price: £49.99

**Free STD consultation**. Worth up to £300 in most private surgeries. Have yours for only £179.99. (Does not include swabs or antibiotics.)

**Selection of unusual and unpleasant smells** to amuse your fellow passengers. Choose any three from: shit, tear gas, burp, bad eggs, vomit, decaying sheep, cow shit, semen, burning rubber, cheesy feet, carbon monoxide, bad breath, bag lady, BO, rotting flesh, elephant shit; each capsule lasts for up to fifty minutes.
Price: £12.99

AVARICE

*By*

SARAH FERGUSON

125cl

**Poisonous Snakes of the World Gift Set**. Be the centre of attention on the plane and at customs. (Includes cage and a week's supply of food.) Choose from: Cobra Combo, Anaconda Action Set and the Black Mamba Medley. Buy two and get a Gila monster for free.
Price: £249.99

**A selection of automatic weapons**. Bullets included. Simply fit together and ready to use. No training necessary. Short range, long range, you name it, easily accessible for all your guerrilla warfare needs.
Prices start from £725.99

A **pen** that will write 4,000 feet underwater and 500,000 miles into space. Press a button on the end and hey presto, a poison-tip arrow shoots out. Be the James Bond of your family. Also contains two suicide pills in case you get caught.
Price: £99.99

**Easy-assemble combine harvester** (weight excluding packaging, 5 tons).
Price: £78,999.99

**His and hers dildo/vibrator/ condom/gel anal sex gift set for on-board dalliances**. Comes complete with 'hideaway', soundproofed 'privacy tent'. Gives new meaning to the phrase 'Come Aboard' from the 3 Miles Low Club.
Price: £64.99

**Hijack kit**: includes flying manual, razor blades, garroting material, a selection of small bombs, door opening device, copy of the Koran, moustaches, coupon for 72 virgins, bolt cutters.
Price: £29.99

Series of **on-board practical jokes**, includes: turd on a seat, panic attack kit, false penis, fake bomb, joke vomit, two-hour recording of Jehovah's Witness; annoy your seat mate with this fake cracked window.
Price: £1.99

**Handy customs smuggling kit**: comes in three sizes for easy insertion up rectum. Undetectable or your money back.
Price: £5.99

**137**

# 70. HARRY POTTER TITLES YOU'LL NEVER SEE (Part 2)

*Harry Potter and the Twisted Testicle*

*Harry Potter and the Half Blood Sausage*

*Harry Potter and the Uncontested Scrums*

*Harry Potter and the Bunch of C\*\*ts*

*Harry Potter vs Predator*

*Harry Potter and the Deadly Tandoori*

*Harry Potter and the Chamber of Commerce*

*Harry Potter and the Silent But Deadly*

*Harry Potter and the Pus-Like Discharge*

*Harry Potter and the Disgusting Smell*

*Harry Potter and the Bag of Skag*

*Harry Potter and the Wet Dream*

*Harry Potter and the Ring of Paedophiles*

*Harry Potter and the Order of the Curry*

# 71. THINGS YOU WOULDN'T READ IN A CHILDREN'S BOOK (Part 2)

And Baby Bear saw Goldilocks sleeping in his bed and jumped in and gave her a second helping of porridge.

'Gruffalo shmufalo,' growled the fox. 'He might like roasted fox but I've got a fucking Kalashnikov.'

Burglar Bill comes to the third building and shines his torch around. 'That's a nice hat and shoes,' he says, putting them into his sack; but then the home owner creeps out and shoots him in the back as he is running away!

'Congratulations, Charlie, you have won the grand prize. You will take over my chocolate factory; well for two weeks anyway, until Kraft launches a hostile takeover.'

'Mr and Mrs Longstocking? We'd like you to come into school and talk about Pippi's mood swings and the white stuff round her nose.'

Chapter One: Janet and John Go Feral.

… and suddenly, Peter Rabbit and all the flopsy bunnies developed Myxomatosis and died horribly.

On Tuesday the very hungry caterpillar ate two doses of pesticide and died in unimaginable agony.

# 72. UNLIKELY NEWS FROM THE BIRTHS AND MARRIAGES PAGES

## ANNOUNCEMENTS

St Andrew's Church: Miranda 'Monkey Face' McGovern married John Rogers yesterday afternoon. Parents 'pinching themselves'.

To their graces the Duke and Duchess of Cambridgeshire, a daughter: Rihanna Chelsea Demi. Big props from the Fen massive.

The marriage between Mary Cock and John Balls takes place at The Church of St John Thomas, Bell End this afternoon and, yes, they know.

Born 6/6/66 to Guy and Rosemary Woodhouse, a son: Adrian. Oh dear.

Hugh JARSE on 14 March at the Portland Hospital to Linda and … oh my God, look what we've done, I hadn't seen it written down before.

Lord and Lady Partington-Smythe ask for the sympathy and condolences of their friends and relatives as they regretfully announce the marriage of their much-loved daughter Wendy to Brian 'T Bone' Shufflebottom.

Baby born yesterday. Not mine. See cheating tart of a wife for further details.

Tommy 'Pre Nup' O'Hara regrets to announce the sudden termination of his engagement to Heather Mills.

Roger Rears and Annie Anal, stars of the film *Backdoor Babes*, are pleased to announce the unexpected birth of their son after an accidental lane change last year.

To the Devil, a daughter.

A child to Wayne and Coleen Rooney, 8 lb 2 oz. Name to be decided after a sitting of the International Commission for Zoological Nomenclature.

Chairman of Network Rail is delighted to announce the arrival of a baby boy, after a twelve-hour delay due to signal failure outside Nuneaton.

Old Widow Johnson celebrates her second marriage at St Peter's Church this afternoon. Congratulations to her first husband.

Mary Jane, born 13 March, look at the pictures, bloody hell they should have a warning on. I thought it was one of those charity appeals.

John 'Shagger' Stevens marries Brenda 'The Bike' Byrne this afternoon. Good luck with that.

Amelie Anais born on 14 April to parents who are clearly middle-class wankers.

Solomon David Asher Cohen born 23 April Golders Green to parents Imran and Shazia.

John Smith, born 14 April, 24 lb 2 oz, father delighted, mother unavailable for comment.

Bethlehem, 25 December: Christ, Jesus H., 7lbs 4 oz to Joseph and Mary of Nazareth near Galilee. He's a little miracle. Gifts welcome but PLEASE, no more myrrh.

8 lbs 3 oz, Garland Streisand Minnelli Smith, born at Brighton Hospital, possibly to a gay couple.

The marriage of multi-billionaire J. Hubert Anderson, 92, and lap dancer Mimi Mounds, 19, took place at his 900-acre estate this weekend. Attendees were limited to fifteen different Anderson family lawyers and Mimi's friend and 'personal trainer' Joaquin 'Turbo' Rodriguez.

12 May 2010. David Cameron and Nick Clegg are delighted to announce their union. The couple won't accept gifts but would be happy to receive voluntary redundancies, overseas aid or donations up to a value of £156 billion.

# 73. UNLIKELY TITLES FOR MEMOIRS (Part 4)

PUTTING ON THE RITZ *by* Jeffrey Dahmer

THE NAKED LUNCH *by* John Prescott and Tracey Temple

I JUST WANT TO BE LEFT ALONE *by* Katie Price

I'M NOT VERY GOOD AT SCORING GOALS *by* Emile Heskey

MY LIFE
(WELL, THE BITS I HAVEN'T ALREADY SOLD TO MAGAZINES)
*by* Kerry Katona

IF YOU'RE READING THIS, I MUST BE DEAD *by* Amy Winehouse

I'M HALF WHITE TOO, REMEMBER *by* Barack Obama

DIANA: HER LIFE SINCE 1997 *by* the Daily Mail

I AM A MAN WHO KICKS A BALL ABOUT
*by* Frank Lampard

RAY STUBBS: THE TRUE STORY

BIRDS, BOOZE AND BOMBS: MY LIFE IN HIDING
*by* Osama bin Laden

MORE THAN A MOUSTACHE *by* Adolf Hitler

# 74. UNLIKELY THINGS TO HEAR ON A PA SYSTEM (Part 2)

'Could the man who has just been decapitated in Coach 6, please stop pressing the emergency button.'

'Ladies and gentlemen, we're now entering the channel with 100 metres of water above us, this elongated coffin, the walls are closing in on me!! Get me out of here!!'

'... where we have teas, coffees, sandwiches, confectionery and an arsenal of weaponry.'

'We are experiencing a delay due to a person under . . . me in my cabin, she's nearly fiiiiiiiinished!!!!'

'Ladies and gentlemen, it's Bring a Child to Work Day today, so this train is currently being driven by my three-year-old daughter, Fifi.'

'There's a broken-down train in the tunnel in front of us so we can expect long delays and ... oh, screw it, who needs a tunnel ... hold on.'

'This is the Age of the Train ... it's about seventy-five, look, it's fucked.'

'Driver, stop saying, "Chuff, chuff, chuff," you're not fooling anyone.'

'This is your driver speaking, we apologise for the delay, this is due to Ivor helping a Soup Dragon to sing at Llaniog.'

'The buffet car is now open for hot and cold water and a selection of breadcrumbs both brown and white.'

'We're going into a tunnel now, woooooo, echo echo echo.'

'Ladies and gentlemen, we have reason to believe there is a beggar on the train, please do not engage him as we operate a shoot on sight policy.'

'The big long hard train will now enter the dark, gaping tunnel. Ooh yeah! Do you like that? Do you? Yeah? Who's the daddy? Take me home.'

'If there are any passengers on board without a valid ticket, please make yourself known to the inspector or else hide in the toilets located in Coaches 3, 6 and 9.'

'Anyone using their mobile phone in this carriage is a c*nt.'

'Oh no, that's an off-peak, blue saver bought on Tuesday, that's not valid, you didn't book in advance online, you just owe us another £10,000.'

'We appear to have taken a wrong turning at Reading and are now on the Piccadilly Line.'

'Welcome aboard the 11.36, calling at Milton Keynes Central, Watford Junction, New York Grand Central, Vladivostock, Timbuktu North, Lapland New Street, Moscow State Circus, the Eighth Ring of Saturn, Warrington Bank Quay and Preston.'

'Passengers not in possession of a ticket will be handed an on the spot £50 fine unless they are bigger then me or prepared to suck me off.'

'Can the two men on the roof please stop fighting to the death until we pull into the next station?'

# 75. UNLIKELY THINGS TO HEAR AT AN AWARDS CEREMONY (Part 2)

'And the winner of the Lifetime Achievement award is: that bloke off *Cash in the Attic!*'

'And the award for the biggest silent fart of the evening goes to: me!'

'Welcome to the 13th Annual Insincere Awards. I can't tell you how thrilled I am to be here.'

'And the next award is for Best Acting Performance for an Actor Hearing the News That They Haven't Won an Award.'

'And the winner of Amputee of the Year, and please give him a big hand, is …'

'Best Actor in a Role for Which They Were Completely Miscast goes to Philip Seymour Hoffman for "Bob the Builder".'

'And the award for Heaviest Woman in a Lead Role goes to …'

'And now the Award that People Will Look Back on in Ten Years' Time and Say, "How the Fuck Did That Win" goes to …'

'And the Nominees for Unfunniest One-Time Comedy Legend are: Woody Allen, Eddie Murphy, Steve Martin and John Cleese.'

'And the award goes to … ooh, ow, paper cut.'

'And the winner of the Longest, Most Drawn-out and Almost Certainly Most Annoying Suspense-Building Applause goes to...'

'Welcome to the Austrian House and Garden Awards. We start with Best Cellar Conversion ...'

'Before all the ones you want to win, the one no one wants to win: Wanker of the Year.'

'Your host for the evening: just Ant.'

'When I see all the other actors who were nominated, I'm frankly not surprised I won.'

'And the nominations for the Hardest Working Man in Showbusiness are: Judy Finnigan's make-up artist, Bruce Forsyth's paramedic team, Fern Britton's arse wrangler and ...'

'And – the – award – for – Best – Auto – Cue – Reader – goes – to – read – name – off – card ...'

'The Hurricane of the Year goes to ... Gustav!'

'And to present this next award, an ugly old boiler'

'We come now to the coveted BAFTA for Best Worthy Drama that Nobody Watched. Jesus, where do we start?'

# 76. UNLIKELY THINGS TO FIND IN AN AUCTION-HOUSE CATALOGUE

**Lot 1:**
Set of crunchy, sperm-encrusted tissues, mint condition, man-sized, reserve price of a penny or nearest offer, would benefit from viewing.

**Lot 2:**
A pair of my old shoes, size ten, comes with free man inside. Buyer collects from my house if I like the look of you through the window.

**Lot 3:**
Premiership football club dating from around 1898 comes with own bell ringer, reserve £1.

**Lot 4:**
Edvard Munch's 'The Scream', as recently seen on *Dickinson's Real Deal*, buyer just wants to beat Dickinson's dealer's offer of £44.

**Lot 5:**
Mobile phones owned by Vernon Kay, Ashley Cole and Tiger Woods, very quick sales, no questions asked.

**Lot 6:**
Original script for BBC sitcom *Life of Riley*, unfortunately very poor quality.

**Lot 7:**
Quantity of top-quality golf clubs, slight damage and blood staining. Vendor Mrs T. Woods (former).

**Lot 8:**
Quality wooden duck house, one rueful owner, take it off my hands, I never want to see the bloody thing again. Yours, Sir Peter Viggers.

**Lot 9:**
Full glass cabinet of Nazi memorabilia, uniforms and weapons. Owner just liked the colours and stuff, honest.

**Lot 10:**
Ancient Etruscan vase with engraving of man with enormous penis shagging woman with massive tits. Well worth viewing even if you have no intention of buying. Phwoar!

**Lot 11:**
Harry Potter's real-life wand, not the one from the film or anything, a real one, you understand. It does real magic. Really works. As verified and signed by the real Dumbledore. Comes with genuine invisibility cloak and real Voldemort death threats.

**Lot 12:**
A limited edition, boxed set of fin-de-siècle dog turds (dating from 1999), ranging in colour from white to black to slightly runny brown (careful when handling and closing lid).

**Lot 13:**
Van Gogh's sunflowers, not the painting, but the actual descendents of the flowers he painted. Reserve £60 million, come on I mean actual sunflowers have to be worth more than just a bloody painting of them.

**Lot 14:**
Cocaine. To street value of £250,000. Not a word to the Fuzz.

**Lot 15:**
100,000 ants in a hollow log. Genuine.

**Lot 16:**
Cup of tea in plastic cup excluding sugar, milk will be supplied. Reserve £1.50.

# 77. LINES CUT FROM THRILLERS

'Take him to the interrogation chamber,' barked the Russian Commander. Though it was never explained how a dog had risen so high in the ranks.

'Let's see who's under that mask. [Pause] Who the fuck are you?'

'These documents must not fall into the hands of a foreign power hostile to our interests. Oh, all right – China.'

'Your mission, Tom Cruise, should you choose to accept it, is to reach the top shelf.'

'Well, Blofeld, I must admit when I saw the plans, I really didn't think the volcano HQ would work – but you've pulled it off and come in under budget.'

He turned over the precision-tooled German-manufactured Glock, and fingered the well-oiled mechanism. He turned to the man next to him. 'Do you have this in red?'

Bond turned towards her. 'Well, after all that flirting, that was something of a disappointment, Moneypenny.'

'Here are your travel documents, Bond. You leave tomorrow, National Express to Slough.'

'It's worse than I thought,' said the doctor, 'it's a virulent new strain of Bacterium Made-up-ium.'

The car hit the road block, flipped into the air and burst into flames before coming to a rest upside down. The sentry stepped forward and shouted, 'Are you paying too much for your car insurance?'

# 78. UNLIKELY VALENTINE'S CARD MESSAGES

*P.S. if you're not interested, please pass this on to your sister*

*Dear David Cameron, you are my one true love, yours, David Cameron*

*To whoever I'm on the cover of Hello with this week – I love you for publicity purposes for a specified period of not less than thirty days subject to contract, yours, Katie P.*

*Loving you gives me a funny feeling in my tummy. Either that or I need a shit*

*I love you to the moon and back. Sorry I can't see you tonight, West Ham are playing*

*I love you despite all your faults, by which I mean your odd-shaped breasts and droopy front bottom*

*I love you, even when it's your wrong time of the month*

*To a smashing sister*

*Please be mine, and remember, if I can't have you,
NO-ONE CAN*

*I bought you some flowers. Well, I had to get petrol anyway*

*Fancy a fuck?*

*I love you so much, I can't go on deceiving you any longer. I'm gay*

*To Fido*

*I want to strip you naked and lick every inch of your body.
P.S. Can you empty the hoover when you've finished and the money's on the side*

**151**

# 79. UNLIKELY COMPLAINTS TO TV NETWORKS

Dear Channel Four, I wish to complain about the awful presenter of your cookery show, *The F-Word*. What a C-word.

Dear Channel Four, I wish to complain about the nudity in last night's French film – it was far too brief, and you couldn't see her muff properly.

Dear Living – call that living?

Dear Auntie Beeb, thank you for the jumper and cheque you sent me for my birthday.

Dear Channel 4 plus one. Why is your clock an hour late?

Dear Bravo, why is your late-night viewing sponsored by Kleenex?

Dear Al-Jazeera, may I say how much I am enjoying your new series, *Strictly No Dancing*.

Dear UK Gold, I've looked up the meaning of the word "gold" and couldn't spot any on your channel.

Dear BBC, there simply aren't enough *Dr Who* spin-off programmes, can't we give Rose Tyler's mum her own series?

Dear BBC, I feel I must complain about your awful programme *Points of View*.

Dear BBC, wouldn't *Hole in the Wall* be better if the walls were made of brick and there was the odd shark in the pool as well?

Dear BBC, why oh why oh why . . . is a dreadful hand at scrabble.

Dear Sir, I feel I should complain in the strongest terms about your programme. I didn't watch it, but I read the *Daily Mail* and they told me to.

Dear *Points of View*, I am an ex-miner from Wales and this doesn't sound like me at all.

Dear BBC, surely *Springwatch* would be much improved if some pitbull terriers were added to the badger set?

Dear BBC, after watching your hit sitcom *Top Gear*, I was struck by an idea – why not get the guys to review cars?

Dear Sky 1, as a bingo fan I was bitterly disappointed by your new programme, *House*.

Dear Dave, I'm sorry but I just don't feel I know you well enough to call you by your first name.

Dear Television X, re: your excellent show, *The Ten-Minute Freeview*. More, please!

Dear Channel 4, I don't enjoy *Countdown* now that Richard Whiteley has left, why don't you bring him back?

# 80. BAD NAMES FOR NEW CHOCOLATE BARS (Part 2)

*Fruit 'n' Nut 'n' Iron Filings*

*Cadbury's Gallstones*

*Snot Mellows*

*Turkish Prison Delight*

*Tapeworm Chews*

*Spunk!*

Brazilian

Black Lung

Rowntree's Foot and Mouth

Family-Size Fritzls

Single Digit of Shortbread
Mechanically Smeared with Viscous
Chocolate-Like Material

Milk Udders

Chocolate Runs

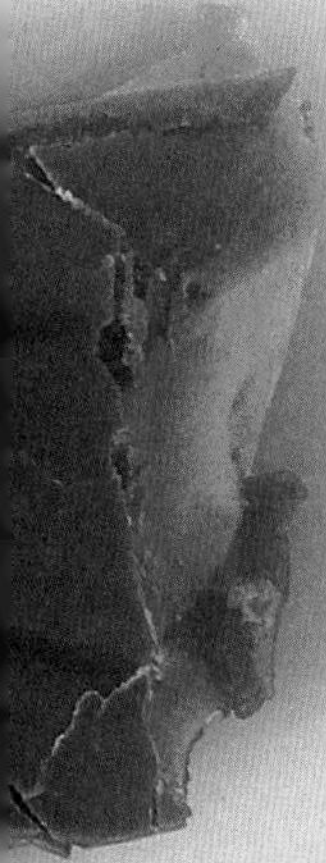

Double Anal

King-Size Chocolate Cock

Marrowbone

Mugabe

Skidmark

Thrush

Chocolate Shower

Tsunami

# 81. UNLIKELY LINES TO HEAR IN A HORROR FILM (Part 2)

'So, finally, Freddy Krueger's dead - he got conjunctivitis and stabbed himself in the eye.'

'I'm sorry but you don't have planning permission for that wicker man, it's going to have to come down.'

'It is the Mummy's curse, it reads: "Don't touch my fucking bandages, you c*nts."'

'I'm Count Dracula - are you by any chance on the blob?'

'And so the lightning comes down from that antenna through these convectors and then into the monster's body, causing his testicles to light up.'

'Van Helsing, I couldn't get hold of any garlic but I've brought some lovely chives.'

'I don't care if you're the creature from the deep, you're not on the list.'

'He's not so much a hound of the Baskervilles, more of a gecko.'

'Because of unexpected snow in Transylvania this flight has been diverted to Luton.'

'I used to be Dracula, but I've become a Buddhist.'

'No, the hunchback left a while back, I'm the Big Fat Bald Guy of Notre Dame.'

'Oh my God, the organ, for God's sake put it away.'

'Dr Frankenstein, are you happy with your current electricity supplier?'

'I think he's dead, why don't we turn our backs on him and have a natter?'

'I can't believe his mother was in the attic! It's like a whole separate granny flat, it's lovely.'

'I know he's just cut your arm off with a chainsaw, but on the plus side you're a dead cert for the 2012 Paralympics.'

'It's alright, I gave Freddie his medication and he's a lot calmer now.'

'Of course you know what I did last summer, I'm a lifeguard.'

# 82. THINGS YOU WOULDN'T EXPECT TO FIND IN AN INDEX

*arse*
  my big fat 240–490
  spotty 490–578
  hairy 578–609
  white and flaky 609–614
  pictures of my 614–720
  did I mention it was spotty?
    720–721
  objects inserted into my
    721–755
  people who have examined my
    755–799
  oh yes, oh yes, I like that, keep
    doing that to my 800–1219

*bin Laden, Osama*
  whereabouts 22
  list of disguises 23
  names and addresses of all
    operatives throughout the
    world 34–35
  erection when I think of him 62

*bit where I tell you the murderer
is Smithers the gamekeeper* 374

*Churchill, Winston*
  early career as lap dancer 34–42
  author of Shakespeare 44–47
  crack habit 52–55
  correspondence concerning
    *Dancing on Ice* 77–79
  toilet habits 102–414
  clubbing holiday in Ayia Napa with
    Harry S. Truman 415–418
  affair with Hitler 419
  tendency to shout, 'Yabba dabba
    doo!' 450–452
  part in Second World War 453

*description of lead character looking
a lot like Matt Damon so I can flog
the film rights* 34–37

*lentils*
  short history of 1–1234
  famous people who like 1234–2345
  contribution to the Battle of
    Agincourt 2345–2347
  people who smell of 2347–2349
  where I normally buy my 2349–2350